I0448444

December 2013

MODERNIZING THE NUCLEAR SECURITY ENTERPRISE

NNSA's Budget Estimates Do Not Fully Align with Plans

December 2013

MODERNIZING THE NUCLEAR SECURITY ENTERPRISE

NNSA's Budget Estimates Do Not Fully Align with Plans

Why GAO Did This Study

Nuclear weapons have been and continue to be an essential part of the nation's defense strategy. The end of the cold war resulted in a shift from designing, testing, and producing new nuclear weapons to maintaining the existing stockpile indefinitely and extending the operational lives of these weapons through refurbishment, without nuclear testing. At the same time, the production infrastructure for nuclear weapons has become outdated.

The National Defense Authorization Act for Fiscal Year 2011 mandated GAO to report annually on whether NNSA's nuclear security budget materials provide for sufficient funding to modernize and refurbish the nuclear security enterprise. This report addresses (1) changes to NNSA's budget estimates for modernizing the nuclear security enterprise since fiscal year 2012 and (2) the extent to which these budget estimates align with NNSA's modernization plans.

To answer these objectives, GAO reviewed NNSA's fiscal year 2012 and 2014 nuclear security budget materials, which are composed of NNSA's budget request justification and its *Stockpile Stewardship and Management Plan*, which describes modernization plans and budget estimates for the next 20 years or longer. GAO also interviewed NNSA and DOD program officials.

What GAO Recommends

GAO recommends that NNSA include a range of budget estimates for preliminary projects and programs in future modernization plans. NNSA generally concurred with the recommendation.

View GAO-14-45. For more information, contact David C. Trimble at (202) 512-3841 or trimbled@gao.gov.

What GAO Found

The National Nuclear Security Administration's (NNSA) total budget estimates for modernizing the nuclear security enterprise for fiscal years 2014 through 2031 have increased by about $19 billion overall when compared with the estimates in the agency's fiscal year 2012 budget materials, with most of the increase occurring in fiscal year 2019 and beyond (see fig.). Factors such as sequestration, the achievability of planned cost savings, and pension liabilities could affect the accuracy of future budget estimates as presented.

Comparison of Budget Estimates for Nuclear Modernization Activities in the National Nuclear Security Administration's 2012 and 2014 Budget Materials

Source: GAO analysis of National Nuclear Security Administration data.

Budget estimates for two of three areas discussed in NNSA's modernization plans may not represent total funding needed and therefore do not fully align with aspects of these plans. In the area of stockpile maintenance and refurbishment, budget estimates increased by $27 billion—accounting for more than the total increase of $19 billion to overall budget estimates for modernization—primarily due to changes in the way that NNSA calculated budget estimates for nuclear weapons refurbishment programs. However, NNSA's plans for two weapons refurbishment programs also indicate that additional funding may be needed before fiscal year 2019 to meet scheduled milestones. In the infrastructure and science, technology, and engineering capabilities areas, NNSA's budget estimates decreased slightly. However, in the infrastructure area, NNSA did not include in its budget estimates billions of dollars in planned major construction projects because officials said these infrastructure plans were too preliminary. Providing Congress with budget estimates that reflect long-term plans and the expected funding needed to execute these plans, even if preliminary, helps in prioritizing projects and funding and aids in congressional decision making.

_____ United States Government Accountability Office

Contents

Figures

Abbreviations

CMRR-NF	Chemistry and Metallurgy Research Replacement Nuclear Facility
DOD	Department of Defense
DOE	Department of Energy
FYNSP	Future-Years Nuclear Security Program
LANL	Los Alamos National Laboratory
LEP	life extension program
LLNL	Lawrence Livermore National Laboratory
NNSA	National Nuclear Security Administration
SNL	Sandia National Laboratories
SSMP	*Stockpile Stewardship and Management Plan*
ST&E	science, technology, and engineering
UPF	Uranium Processing Facility

December 11, 2013

Congressional Committees

Nuclear weapons have been and continue to be an essential part of the nation's defense strategy. Since 1992, the United States has observed a moratorium on underground testing of nuclear weapons. During the cold war, the nation designed, tested, and produced new nuclear weapons. Since then, the strategy has shifted to maintaining the existing nuclear weapons stockpile indefinitely by extending the operational lives of these weapons through refurbishment, without nuclear testing. The Department of Energy's (DOE) National Nuclear Security Administration (NNSA)[1] is responsible for activities in pursuit of this mission, which is largely executed at eight government-owned, contractor-operated sites that comprise its nuclear security enterprise.[2] This science-based approach to stockpile stewardship has ensured a credible U.S. nuclear deterrent without full-scale nuclear testing.

After the cold war, the production infrastructure of the nuclear security enterprise had aged and became outdated. The 2001 *Nuclear Posture Review* found that the nuclear weapons manufacturing infrastructure had atrophied and needed to be repaired.[3] The review also called for the development of a "responsive infrastructure" that would support a smaller nuclear deterrent. NNSA's Complex Transformation effort in the mid-

---

[1]NNSA is a separately organized agency within DOE that is responsible for the management and security of DOE's nuclear weapons, nuclear nonproliferation, and naval reactor programs.

[2]NNSA oversees three national nuclear weapons design laboratories—Lawrence Livermore National Laboratory in California, Los Alamos National Laboratory in New Mexico, and Sandia National Laboratories in New Mexico and California. It also oversees four nuclear weapons production plants—the Pantex Plant in Texas, the Y-12 National Security Complex in Tennessee, the Kansas City Plant in Missouri, and tritium operations at DOE's Savannah River Site in South Carolina. NNSA also oversees the Nevada National Security Site, formerly known as the Nevada Test Site.

[3]Section 1041 of the Floyd D. Spence Defense Authorization Act for Fiscal Year 2001 (Pub. L. No. 106-398) required the Secretary of Defense, in consultation with the Secretary of Energy, to "conduct a comprehensive review of the nuclear posture of the United States for the next 5 to 10 years." The 2001 *Nuclear Posture Review* was the second post-cold war review of U.S. strategic nuclear forces. The first one was conducted in 1994.

2000s sought to transform the nuclear security enterprise into a smaller, more efficient enterprise that could respond to changing national security challenges.[4] The 2010 *Nuclear Posture Review* built on these efforts by identifying long-term modernization goals and requirements, including sustaining a safe, secure, and effective nuclear arsenal through the life extension of existing nuclear weapons; increasing investments to rebuild and modernize the nation's nuclear infrastructure; and strengthening the science, technology, and engineering (ST&E) base.[5] To meet these modernization goals, NNSA is refurbishing weapons in the stockpile to extend their operational lives; replacing or renovating research, development, and production facilities that date back to the 1940s and 1950s; performing simulations and laboratory experiments to ensure existing nuclear weapons remain safe and reliable; and recruiting and training personnel with the specialized skills to sustain the nation's nuclear weapons program and maintain the stockpile into the future.[6] In addition to NNSA, two other organizations are responsible for the nation's nuclear weapons program. First, the Department of Defense (DOD) is responsible for implementing the U.S. nuclear deterrent strategy, which includes establishing the military requirements associated with planning for the stockpile.[7] Second, the Nuclear Weapons Council is a joint activity composed of representatives from DOD and DOE that facilitates high-level coordination to secure, maintain, and sustain the nuclear weapons stockpile.

---

[4]73 Fed. Reg. 77,644 (Dec. 19, 2008), 73 Fed. Reg. 77,656 (Dec. 19, 2008), and National Nuclear Security Administration, *Final Complex Transformation Supplemental Programmatic Environmental Impact Statement*, DOE/EIS-0236-S4 (Washington, D.C.: October 2008).

[5]Department of Defense, *Nuclear Posture Review Report* (Washington, D.C.: Apr. 6, 2010).

[6]NNSA's efforts to improve its operations and business practices predate the 2010 *Nuclear Posture Review* but are now considered part of NNSA's modernization efforts.

[7]Additional information on DOD's roles and responsibilities for nuclear weapons is discussed in GAO, *ICBM Modernization: Approaches to Basing Options and Interoperable Warhead Designs Need Better Planning and Synchronization*, GAO-13-831 (Washington, D.C.: Sept. 20, 2013).

NNSA's modernization plans and budget estimates[8] are described in two key policy documents, updated annually, that together comprise NNSA's nuclear security budget materials.[9] First, NNSA's *Stockpile Stewardship and Management Plan* (SSMP) provides information on modernization and operations plans and budget estimates over the next 25 years.[10] The SSMP is NNSA's formal means for communicating to Congress the status of certain activities and its long-range plans and budget estimates for sustaining the stockpile and modernizing the nuclear security enterprise. The SSMP also discusses the current and projected composition and condition of the nuclear weapons stockpile. NNSA has submitted annual reports to meet current or similar previous statutory requirements since

---

[8]NNSA refers to the cost figures included in its budget materials during the FYNSP period as "budget requirements" and those after the FYNSP as "estimated budget requirements." We refer to these figures as "budget estimates" throughout this report.

[9]A third document that includes information on modernization budget estimates is the annual report DOD and DOE are required to submit jointly to the relevant Senate and House committees and subcommittees, referred to as the "section 1043" report. DOD and DOE are required to submit a detailed report that addresses, among other things, the plan for the nuclear weapons stockpile and its delivery systems and a 10-year estimate of modernization budget estimates. (Pub. L. No. 112-81, § 1043 (2011).) The 2014 report contains information through 2023 that appears consistent with NNSA's other budget materials. As required by law, GAO is reviewing the accuracy and completeness of the budget estimates published in the 2014 report in another engagement. The law requires GAO to summarize its review 180 days after the issuance of the section 1043 report, which was issued in July 2013.

[10]NNSA expanded the time span included in the SSMP from 20 years in the 2012 SSMP to 25 years in the 2014 SSMP.

1998, with the exception of 2013.[11] NNSA's 2014 SSMP contains information, including budget estimates, on modernization plans through 2038. These data reflect the budget estimates for the 2014 to 2018 Future-Years Nuclear Security Program (FYNSP), as well as long-range budget estimates through 2038. Second, NNSA's annual justification of the President's budget request, which typically includes the FYNSP, provides program information and budget estimates for the next 5 years and is approved by the Office of Management and Budget.[12] The President's budget is a statement of the President's policy priorities. The President's budget, though not legally binding, provides Congress with recommended spending levels for programs, projects, and activities, based on these priorities. Once the President has submitted the budget, agency officials explain and justify the request to Congress, including through their written budget request justifications. NNSA's fiscal year 2014 budget request justification and FYNSP provide information and estimates through fiscal year 2018.[13] The *GAO Cost Estimating and Assessment Guide* states that a competent estimate is the foundation of a budget because a reasonable and supportable budget is essential to a program's efficient and timely execution.[14] Additionally, credible cost

---

[11]Department of Energy, *Fiscal Year 2014 Stockpile Stewardship and Management Plan Report to Congress,* (Washington, D.C.: June 2013). The National Defense Authorization Act for Fiscal Year 1998 required DOE to develop and annually update a plan for the stewardship, management, and certification of the nuclear weapons stockpile and submit it to Congress. Starting in 1998, NNSA submitted an annual *Stockpile Stewardship Plan* (also known as the "Green Book"). In 2011, a presidential memorandum directed DOD and DOE to jointly submit annual updates to the plan. The National Defense Authorization Act for Fiscal Year 2013 requires NNSA, in consultation with DOD, to develop and annually update the nuclear weapons stockpile stewardship, management, and infrastructure plan but to submit to congressional defense committees a detailed report on the plan in odd-numbered years and summaries of the plan in even-numbered years. *See* 50 U.S.C. § 2523. The 2014 SSMP states that NNSA did not submit the 2013 SSMP to Congress because analytic work conducted by DOD and NNSA to evaluate the out-year needs for nuclear modernization activities across the nuclear security enterprise was ongoing and, as such, predecisional. According to the 2013 budget request justification, out-year data for Weapons Activities it contains do not reflect programmatic requirements. Instead, they are an extrapolation of the 2013 request based on rates of inflation in the Budget Control Act of 2011 (Pub. L. No. 112-25 (2011)).

[12]Pub. L. No. 106-65, § 3253 (1999), as amended, requires NNSA to submit a FYNSP "at or about the time the President's budget is submitted to Congress."

[13]All years in this report refer to fiscal years, unless otherwise noted.

[14]GAO, *GAO Cost Estimating and Assessment Guide: Best Practices for Developing and Managing Capital Program Costs (Supersedes GAO-07-1134SP),* GAO-09-3SP (Washington, D.C.: Mar. 2, 2009).

estimates help program offices justify budgets to Congress, the Office of Management and Budget, department secretaries, and others.

The National Defense Authorization Act for Fiscal Year 2011 mandated that GAO study and report annually on whether NNSA's nuclear security budget materials provide for funding that is sufficient to modernize and refurbish the nuclear security enterprise.[15] This is the third year that we have undertaken work in response to this mandate. In June 2011, we briefed you on our findings based on NNSA's 2012 nuclear security budget materials. We found, among other things, that NNSA's 2012 budget justification and associated FYNSP generally supported the agency's long-range plans, but that a number of issues could affect these plans. These issues included the management of major construction projects without firm cost and schedule baselines, which could lead to project cost growth and schedule slippages that might adversely affect NNSA's modernization plans, as well as challenges in refurbishing weapons using aging infrastructure. In June 2012, we sent a letter to the Senate and House Armed Services Committees that explained that we could not complete our review of the 2013 budget materials because NNSA did not issue the documents required for our review. This report assesses (1) changes to NNSA's budget estimates for modernizing the nuclear security enterprise from the 2012 budget materials to the 2014 materials and (2) the extent to which the 2014 budget estimates align with its long-range modernization plans.

To address these objectives, we reviewed NNSA's 2014 nuclear security budget materials. Specifically, to determine the changes to NNSA's plans and budget estimates, we compared the information in the 2014 budget materials to the information in the 2012 versions of these materials. Those budget materials include information for different time frames (see fig. 1). Because the budget materials for 2012 and 2014 each include information for 2014 through 2031, we focused on these years in our comparative analysis. To determine the extent to which NNSA's budget estimates align with its long-range plans, we compared the data on budget estimates in the 2014 budget materials with the information on long-range plans in the same documents. We discussed perceived

---

[15]Pub. L. No. 111-383, § 3113 (2011), *as amended by* Pub. L. No. 112-239, § 3132(a)(2) (2013).

misalignments with NNSA officials, as well as officials from a DOD office with knowledge of NNSA's modernization plans and budget estimates.

Figure 1: Time Frames Covered by the 2012 and 2014 National Nuclear Security Administration's Nuclear Security Budget Materials

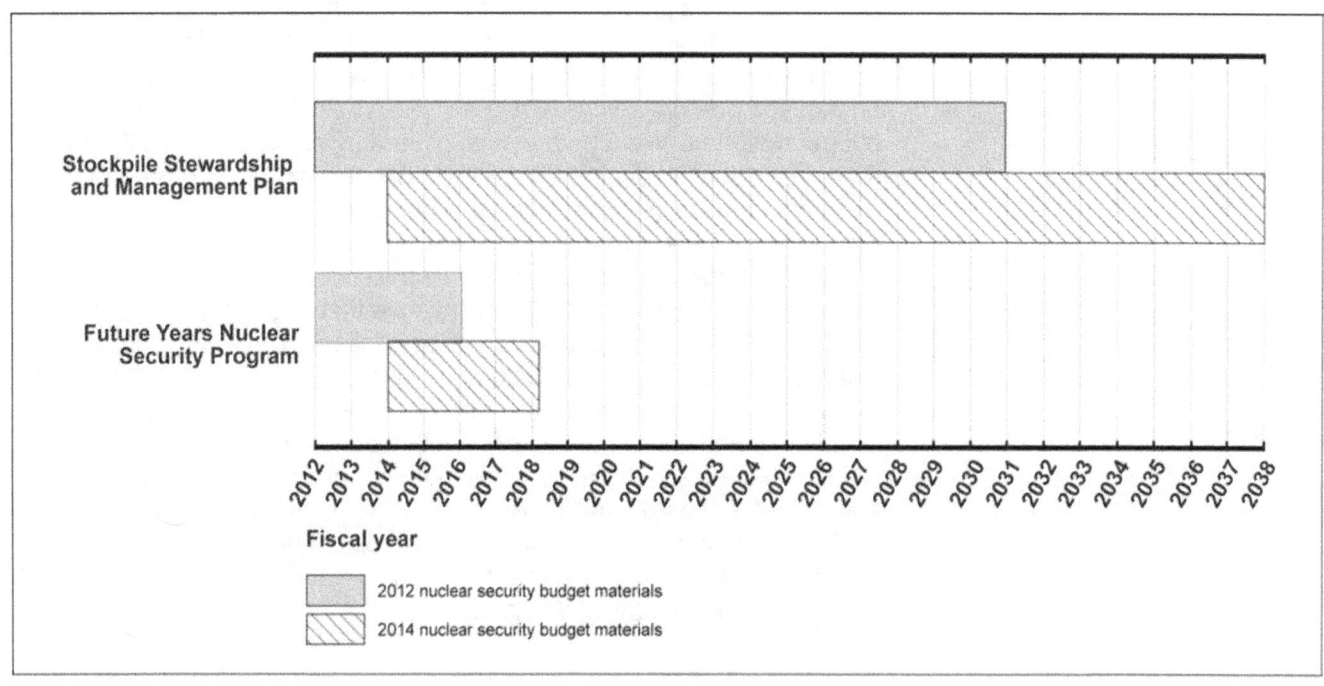

Source: GAO analysis of National Nuclear Security Administration data.

Additionally, we reviewed prior GAO reports on modernization and the specific programs or projects included in NNSA's modernization plans, as well as the *GAO Cost Estimating and Assessment Guide*.[16] A list of related GAO products is included at the end of this report. We limited the scope of our review to NNSA's Weapons Activities appropriation.[17] NNSA does not have a definition of modernization, but an NNSA official

---

[16]GAO-09-3SP.

[17]NNSA's budget consists of four appropriations: (1) Defense Nuclear Nonproliferation, (2) Naval Reactors, (3) Office of the Administrator, and (4) Weapons Activities. The 2014 budget request for all four appropriations totaled $11.7 billion, with $7.9 billion—or 68 percent—requested for Weapons Activities.

responsible for the SSMP told us the agency considers all of the programs in the Weapons Activities appropriation to directly or indirectly support modernization, and NNSA structures its budget materials in that way. This approach is consistent with our June 2011 review of NNSA's 2012 budget materials. Additionally, we focused our review for this report on those programs or projects with the potential to have a significant impact on NNSA's modernization plans or budgets due to the amount of the budget estimates or the importance of the program to NNSA's mission. All data are presented in current dollars unless otherwise noted. To assess the reliability of the data underlying NNSA's budget estimates, we reviewed the data to identify missing items, outliers, or obvious errors; interviewed knowledgeable NNSA officials about the data and their methodologies for using the data to construct their estimates; and compared the figures in the budget request justification with those in the 2014 SSMP to ensure that they were consistent. We determined that the data were sufficiently reliable for our purposes. See appendix I for additional information on the scope and methodology of our review.

We conducted this performance audit from April 2013 to December 2013 in accordance with generally accepted government auditing standards. Those standards require that we plan and perform the audit to obtain sufficient, appropriate evidence to provide a reasonable basis for our findings and conclusions based on our audit objectives. We believe that the evidence obtained provides a reasonable basis for our findings and conclusions based on our audit objectives.

Background

In recent years, U.S. nuclear weapons policy has been focused on arms reduction to address current security challenges posed by the threats of nuclear terrorism and nuclear proliferation. According to the 2010 *Nuclear Posture Review*, changes in the international nuclear security environment, including an easing of cold war rivalries and a growth in U.S. conventional military capabilities, enable the United States to address these security challenges at lower nuclear force levels and with reduced reliance on nuclear weapons.[18] The 2010 *Nuclear Posture Review* focused on five objectives for U.S. nuclear weapons policy, including reducing the role of nuclear weapons in national security strategy and maintaining strategic deterrence and stability at reduced

---

[18]Department of Defense, *Nuclear Posture Review Report* (Washington, D.C.: April 2010).

nuclear force levels. In the New Strategic Arms Reduction Treaty between the United States and Russia, which was ratified by the United States Senate in December 2010, the United States agreed to reduce the number of deployed strategic nuclear warheads to 1,550 by 2018. In June 2013, the President announced new guidance on the use of nuclear weapons. According to the announcement, the guidance includes, among other things, a narrowing of the nuclear strategy to focus only on those objectives and missions that are necessary for deterrence, which further reduces the role of nuclear weapons in the U.S. security strategy.

As the United States reduces its nuclear stockpile, the administration has pledged additional funds to modernize and operate the nuclear security enterprise, including the refurbishment of weapons currently in the stockpile and construction of replacement research and production facilities to support these refurbishments. This increased investment in the nuclear security enterprise is intended to ensure that scientific, technical, and engineering capabilities are sufficiently supported such that a smaller nuclear deterrent continues to be safe, secure, and reliable.[19] Ensuring that the nuclear weapons stockpile remains safe and reliable in the absence of underground nuclear testing is extraordinarily complicated and requires state-of-the-art experimental and computing facilities, as well as the skills of top scientists and engineers in the field.

Congress funds NNSA's modernization efforts through various activities and programs within the Weapons Activities appropriation that generally address three areas: (1) stockpile, (2) infrastructure, and (3) ST&E capabilities. Our review of NNSA's nuclear security budget materials also focuses on these three areas as follows:

- *Stockpile*. The stockpile area includes weapons refurbishment through life extension programs (LEP) and other major weapons alterations

---

[19]DOD and DOE have established an annual assessment process that reaches conclusions and makes judgments about the U.S. nuclear stockpile and, in particular, whether it is necessary to conduct an underground nuclear test to resolve any questions about a particular weapon type. The annual assessment process takes about 14 months to complete, during which time the nuclear weapons community collaborates on technical issues affecting the safety, reliability, performance, and military effectiveness of the stockpile. The process culminates in the "Report on Stockpile Assessments" provided to the President by the Secretaries of Defense and Energy. See GAO, *Nuclear Weapons: Annual Assessment of the Safety, Performance, and Reliability of the Nation's Stockpile*, GAO-07-243R (Washington, D.C.: Feb. 2, 2007).

and modifications;[20] surveillance efforts to evaluate the condition, safety, and reliability of stockpiled weapons; maintenance efforts to perform certain minor weapons alterations or to replace components that have limited lifetimes; and core activities to support these efforts, such as maintaining base capabilities to produce uranium and plutonium weapons components.[21] The U.S. nuclear weapons stockpile is composed of seven different weapon types, including air-delivered bombs, ballistic missile warheads, and cruise missile warheads (see table 1). Most types of nuclear weapons currently in the stockpile were produced more than 20 years ago and are being sustained beyond their original design lifetimes. Consequently, it is critical to ensure that the weapons in the nuclear stockpile are safe, secure, and reliable. Based on our analysis of NNSA's data, an average of about 55 percent of the budget estimates for the stockpile area from 2014 to 2038 is budgeted directly for the LEPs.

Table 1: Types of Nuclear Weapons

Warhead or bomb type	Description	Life extension program or major alteration planned from 2014 to 2038
B61-3/4/10	Tactical bomb	X[a]
B61-7/11	Strategic bomb	
W76-0/1	Submarine-launched ballistic missile warhead	X
W78	Intercontinental ballistic missile warhead	X[b]
W80-1	Air Launched Cruise Missile, Advanced Cruise Missile	X
B83-0/1	Strategic bomb	
W87	Intercontinental ballistic missile warhead	X[c]
W88	Submarine-launched ballistic missile warhead	X[b]

Source: Nuclear Weapons Council.

[a]NNSA is consolidating the 3, 4, 7, and 10 modifications of the B61 bomb into a single B61-12 modification during an ongoing life extension program.

[20]LEPs extend, through refurbishment, the operational lives of weapons in the nuclear stockpile by 20 to 30 years and certify these weapons' military performance requirements without underground nuclear testing.

[21]NNSA funds activities that directly support the stockpile area through the Directed Stockpile Work program within the Weapons Activities appropriation.

[b]NNSA plans to perform a major alteration of the W88, as well as a subsequent life extension program for the W78/88-1, which is planned to become the first interoperable warhead.

[c]NNSA plans to refurbish the W87 as part of a future interoperable warhead LEP.

- *Infrastructure.* The infrastructure area involves NNSA-owned, leased, and permitted physical infrastructure and facilities required to support weapons activities.[22] NNSA's 2014 nuclear security budget materials include information on budget estimates for two types of infrastructure activities: funding to operate and maintain the existing infrastructure, and funding to construct new facilities or modernize existing ones. Based on our analysis of NNSA's budget materials, an average of about 60 percent of the budget estimates for infrastructure from 2014 to 2038 is for the operation and maintenance of existing facilities and about 25 percent is for facilities construction.[23]

- *ST&E capabilities.* The ST&E capabilities area is composed of five "campaigns," which are technically challenging, multiyear, multifunctional efforts to develop and maintain critical science and engineering capabilities, including capabilities that enable the annual assessment of the safety and reliability of the stockpile, improve understanding of the physics and materials science associated with nuclear weapons, extend nuclear weapon lifetimes, and support the development of code-based models that replace underground testing. The five campaigns through which Congress funds ST&E capabilities are the following:

---

[22]In the 2014 budget request justification, the administration has requested that Congress fund activities that support the infrastructure area through the Nuclear Programs and Site Stewardship programs within the Weapons Activities appropriation. Congress has traditionally directed funding for infrastructure activities primarily through NNSA's Readiness in Technical Base and Facilities program within the Weapons Activities Appropriation. The committee report accompanying the House of Representatives' 2014 Energy and Water Development appropriations bill retains the Readiness in Technical Base and Facilities program rather than using the new structure identified in NNSA's budget request justification for 2014. The committee report accompanying the Senate bill, on the other hand, supported NNSA's efforts to restructure the former Readiness in Technical Base and Facilities program. Because we reviewed NNSA's plans in its budget materials, and these documents use the revised account structure, we refer to the accounts described in NNSA's nuclear security budget materials.

[23]The remaining portion is for activities funded through program accounts that are not directly related to infrastructure, such as the Minority Serving Institutions Partnership Program—one of NNSA's outreach programs with universities—and the Material Recycling and Recovery subprogram, which provides recycling and recovery of plutonium, enriched uranium, lithium, and tritium from fabrication and assembly operations, limited life components, and dismantlement of weapons and components.

- The Advanced Simulation and Computing Campaign procures supercomputers, develops the computer code to simulate nuclear weapons, and develops the simulations to analyze and predict these weapons' performance, safety, and reliability and to certify their functionality.
- The Engineering Campaign develops capabilities to assess and improve the safety, security, effectiveness, and performance of a nuclear weapon throughout its lifetime without further underground nuclear testing. The campaign matures technologies for maintaining the current stockpile and adapts technologies for future use. It also provides a fundamental research, development, and engineering basis for stockpile certification and assessment throughout the entire life cycle of each weapon.
- The Inertial Confinement Fusion Ignition and High Yield Campaign utilizes laser- and pulsed power-based high energy density physics to enhance scientific understanding and advanced experimental capabilities to study materials under extreme conditions similar to those of a nuclear explosion.
- The Readiness Campaign develops and deploys capabilities to meet current and future nuclear weapon design and production needs of the stockpile, including tritium, a key isotope of hydrogen used in nuclear weapons.
- The Science Campaign conducts scientific experiments to improve the reliability of physics models for weapons performance. The campaign supports, among other things, annual stockpile assessments, the development of predictive capability in weapons simulations, and experiments to understand the complexities associated with the extreme temperatures, stresses, strains, and strain rates experienced during a nuclear explosion.

The three areas involved in NNSA's modernization efforts are interconnected. For example, performance of research and experiments funded in the ST&E area contribute to the design and production of refurbished weapons, funded in the stockpile area. The infrastructure area offers critical support to both the stockpile and ST&E capabilities areas by providing a suitable environment for their various activities, such as producing weapons components and performing research and experimentation activities.[24]

NNSA uses a system of planning, programming, budgeting, and evaluation to develop its annual budget requests and to plan for future budget requests.[25] The future requests evolve each year based on changes to the programs and policy decisions. NNSA worked with DOD's Office of Cost Assessment and Program Evaluation starting in 2012 to determine the resources needed to accomplish NNSA's nuclear weapons program and recapitalize its infrastructure due to concerns raised by senior DOD and NNSA officials about the sufficiency of NNSA's 2012 budget request to execute its program objectives. This analysis informed NNSA's planning and programming decisions for 2014 through 2018 and will serve as the foundation for future budget requests. In May 2013, NNSA announced the creation of its Office of Program Review and Analysis to improve the agency's ability to budget and plan, as well as to increase accountability for programmatic goals. Going forward, this office is expected to perform some of the same roles as DOD's Office of Cost Assessment and Program Evaluation performed in developing the 2014 budget materials.

Total Budget Estimates for Modernization Have Increased, but the Estimates May Not Be Fully Accurate

NNSA's total budget estimates for modernization for 2014 through 2031 have increased by about $19 billion overall when compared with the estimate in the 2012 budget materials for the same time period. However, three factors may affect whether the estimates accurately reflect the amount NNSA may request in the future: (1) the estimates do not incorporate reductions for sequestration, (2) NNSA incorporated cost savings into its budget estimates before assessing how to achieve the savings, and (3) NNSA may continue to face pressure to pay the increasing costs of legacy contractor pensions.

---

[24]Other programmatic efforts that NNSA does not consider as part of its modernization efforts also depend on nuclear weapons infrastructure and ST&E capabilities. These include, for example, NNSA's Nuclear Counterterrorism Incident Response program, which responds to and mitigates nuclear and radiological incidents worldwide.

[25]GAO, *Modernizing the Nuclear Security Enterprise: NNSA's Reviews of Budget Estimates and Decisions on Resource Trade-offs Need Strengthening*, GAO-12-806 (Washington, D.C.: July 31, 2012).

NNSA's total budget estimates for modernization from 2014 through 2031 have increased from about $169 billion in the 2012 budget materials to about $188 billion in the 2014 budget materials—a net increase of about $19 billion (see table 2).[26] Budget estimates for the stockpile area increased significantly, while budget estimates for the infrastructure and ST&E capabilities areas decreased slightly. Reasons for these differences are discussed below.

Table 2: Changes in the National Nuclear Security Administration's Budget Estimates for Modernization for 2014 to 2031

Dollars in billions

Area	2012 nuclear security budget materials	2014 nuclear security budget materials	Difference
Stockpile	$46.0	$73.1	$27.1
Infrastructure	54.6	52.4	-2.2
Science, technology, and engineering capabilities	40.1	36.2	-3.9
All other weapons activities	28.0	26.2	-1.7
Total	**$168.7**	**$187.9**	**$19.2**

Source: GAO analysis of National Nuclear Security Administration data.

Note: Totals may not sum due to rounding.

Further, the increase in budget estimates through 2031 does not appear until 2019 (see fig. 2). For the 5 years of the FYNSP (2014 to 2018), NNSA's annual budget estimates for modernization are similar in the 2012 budget materials and the 2014 budget materials. However, starting in 2019, NNSA's budget estimates increase more significantly than was anticipated in its 2012 budget materials. The 2014 SSMP states that the long-range estimates are snapshots in time based on expected inflation and other anticipated programmatic factors. In the budget estimates beyond 2018, NNSA incorporated an automatic increase of 2 percent per year to account for inflation for those activities that were expected to continue to operate at the same level of effort as during the FYNSP period. For programs, such as the LEPs, or other discrete projects that

---

[26]The 2012 nuclear security budget materials stated that NNSA's budget estimates for 2012 through 2031 totaled $184 billion. The 2014 SSMP includes budget estimates through 2038. NNSA's total budget estimates for 2014 through 2038 total $276 billion.

are not expected to continue to operate at the same level, NNSA
estimated the funding needed using available planning data.

**Figure 2: Comparison of Budget Estimates for Nuclear Modernization Activities in the National Nuclear Security
Administration's 2012 and 2014 Budget Materials**

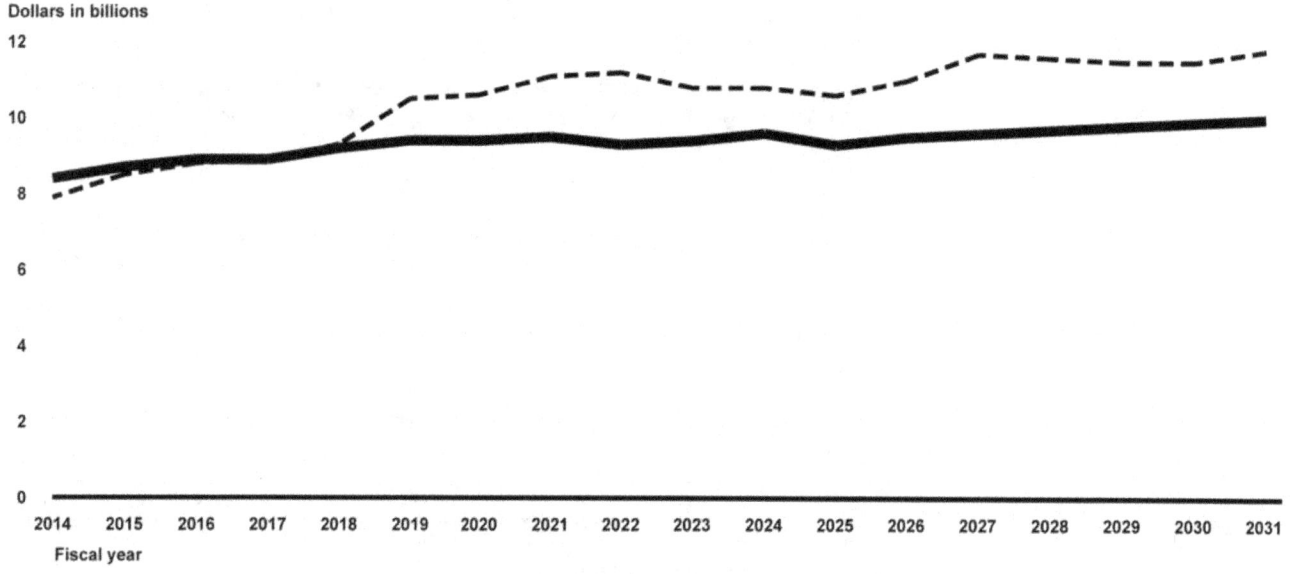

Dollars in billions

Fiscal year

■■■■ 2012 nuclear security budget materials
▬ ▬ ▬ 2014 nuclear security budget materials

Source: GAO analysis of National Nuclear Security Administration data.

Notes: Data are presented in current dollars.

In its 2014 budget materials, the National Nuclear Security Administration (NNSA) proposed moving
funding for the Nuclear Counterterrorism Incident Response and National Security Applications
programs to the Defense Nuclear Nonproliferation appropriation. NNSA included budget estimates for
these activities as part of modernization funding in the 2012 budget materials but not in the 2014
budget materials. We were not able to remove this funding from the data above in the 2012 line.
NNSA spent a total of about $230 million for these programs in 2012, the most recent year for which
data are available.

Three factors may affect whether the estimates accurately reflect the
amounts NNSA may request in the future, particularly with respect to the
budgetary resources that may be needed for specific years: (1) the
estimates do not incorporate reductions for sequestration, (2) NNSA
incorporated cost savings into its budget estimates before assessing how
to achieve the savings, and (3) NNSA may continue to face pressure to
pay the increasing costs of certain contractor pensions. Additional
information on issues related to the accuracy of budget estimates for the
stockpile area and infrastructure areas are discussed in those sections.

First, NNSA's budget estimates do not incorporate reductions for sequestration because, according to an NNSA official, the 2014 budget request and future budget estimates reflect the total amount of funding needed for the programs to meet their current plans and schedules. As indicated in the 2014 SSMP, the plan represents the requirements for the modernization of the nuclear security enterprise. According to the SSMP, incorporating reductions for sequestration would lead to adjustments to future plans. This could include changes to current plans and schedules. Additionally, according to NNSA officials, sequestration occurred at about the same time as the agency submitted its 2014 budget request to Congress. While NNSA did not submit the 2014 SSMP to Congress until June, NNSA did not update its budget estimates because the officials said the SSMP was supposed to be consistent with the 2014 budget request.

Second, NNSA incorporated cost savings into its budget estimates before fully assessing how to achieve the savings. An NNSA official said that the Office of Management and Budget directed NNSA to incorporate these cost savings into its budget estimates to reduce the total top-line estimates. NNSA's budget estimates incorporate about $24 billion in cost savings to be achieved through management efficiencies and workforce prioritization savings through 2038, including $320 million in 2014. According to NNSA officials, management efficiencies reflect changes in business processes that are not expected to affect the scope of work that can be completed. However, work scope is expected to be affected as a result of workforce prioritization savings because these savings result from reducing the size of the workforce and shifting personnel from lower priority work to higher priority work. Figure 3 shows the reductions that NNSA incorporated into its budget estimates for management efficiencies and workforce prioritization for 2014 through 2038.

Figure 3: Amount of the Reductions That the National Nuclear Security Administration Incorporated into its Budget Estimates for Management Efficiencies and Workforce Prioritization Savings

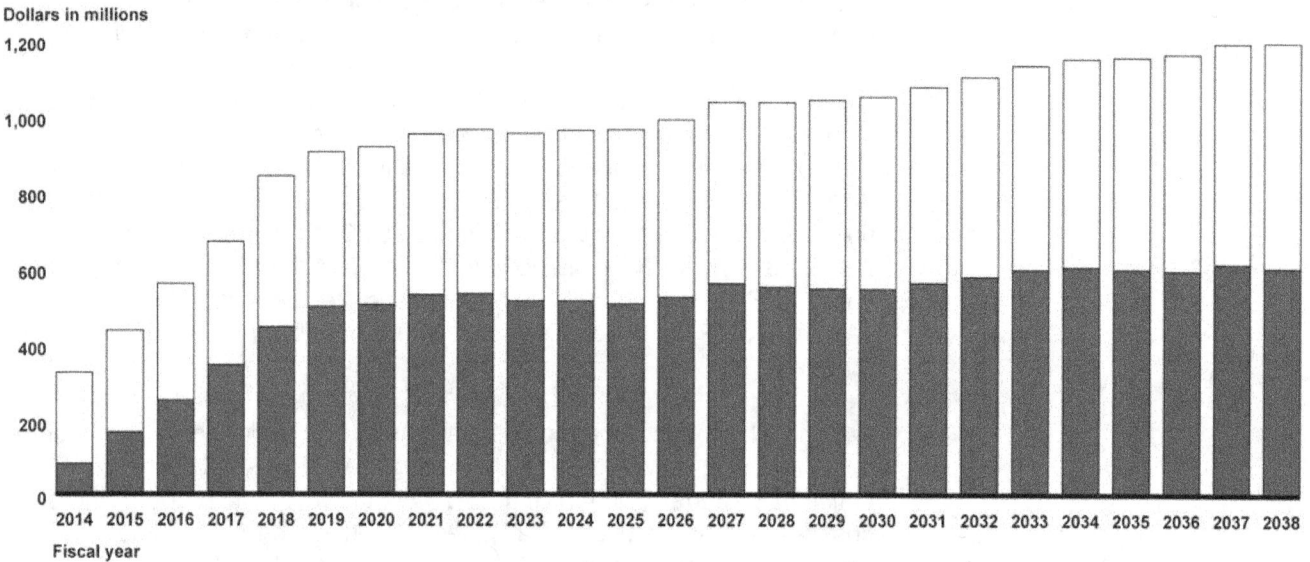

Source: GAO analysis of National Nuclear Security Administration data

Note: Data are presented in current dollars.

Shortly after issuing its budget materials, NNSA began studies to identify how to achieve these cost savings and whether they could be achieved. According to NNSA officials, they completed the workforce prioritization study in November 2013 and had not completed the management efficiencies study as of December 2013.[27] Because NNSA's 2014 budget materials were released before the agency completed its studies, an NNSA official said that the anticipated cost savings for management efficiencies and workforce prioritization reductions were evenly distributed across the programs that support modernization efforts. According to NNSA's 2014 budget request justification and information from NNSA officials, NNSA plans to work with Congress to make any necessary

---

[27]We did not review NNSA's workforce prioritization report because it was issued so close to the completion of our audit work. We plan to review the report as part of our future reviews of the SSMP.

GAO-14-45 Modernizing the Nuclear Security Enterprise

changes to programs and funding levels after these studies are complete.[28]

NNSA officials said that incorporating the workforce prioritization savings will require a reduction in some planned activities, as implementing these savings will lead to fewer employees available to perform the work. According to the 2014 SSMP, NNSA's workforce includes about 30,000 contractor employees across the nuclear security enterprise and about 2,300 federal employees directly employed by NNSA. About 88 percent of the contractor workforce supports programs NNSA considers modernization activities. Based on preliminary results of the workforce prioritization study, NNSA officials said that they expect that the highest priority work will be the LEPs and that surveillance[29] and engineering activities that are not directly related to ongoing LEPs would most likely be cut to achieve $240 million in workforce prioritization savings for 2014 and additional savings in future years.[30] According to an NNSA official, this trade-off is necessary because the people who perform surveillance and engineering activities have the skills to support LEPs, while other

---

[28]Section 3116 of the House version of the National Defense Authorization Act for Fiscal Year 2014, if enacted, would limit NNSA's ability to obligate $139.5 million of the funds authorized to be appropriated in the act or otherwise made available for the fiscal year until NNSA submits to the relevant Senate and House committees a detailed plan to realize the planned efficiencies described in the President's 2014 budget request and a written certification that the planned efficiencies will be achieved during 2014. In addition, if NNSA does not submit the plan and certification within 60 days of the enactment of the act, NNSA must submit to congressional defense committees the amount of planned efficiencies that will not be realized during 2014 and any effects caused by the unrealized planned efficiencies to the Nuclear Programs and Directed Stockpile Work programs.

[29]NNSA's surveillance program provides data to evaluate the condition of the active and inactive stockpile to support decisions regarding weapon alterations or modifications; life extensions; and assessments of reliability, safety, security, and performance of the stockpile.

[30]To put this figure in context, based on an average annual total compensation of about $150,000 for a full-time employee, saving $240 million from workforce prioritization reductions could mean a reduction of about 1,600 positions. For this calculation, we obtained data on average salary and benefits for DOE employees. Although positions eliminated due to workforce prioritization reductions are more likely to be contractors than government employees, information on average salaries for the management and operations contractors was not readily available. If contractor salaries are higher than the data used in our calculation, then fewer positions would need to be eliminated. If contractor salaries are lower than the data used in our calculation, then more positions would need to be eliminated. See appendix I for more information on the methodology used for our calculation.

knowledge, skills, and abilities dedicated to other efforts within the nuclear security enterprise cannot be readily redirected to support LEPs. However, according to NNSA officials, NNSA could choose to allocate the savings differently to avoid impacts to other programs.

A third factor affecting the overall accuracy of NNSA's budget estimates is that NNSA is responsible for contributing to the pensions of certain employees and annuitants of the University of California who worked as contractors for NNSA until the mid-2000s. NNSA's budget estimates for legacy contractor pensions increase across the FYNSP and post-FYNSP periods to nearly $360 million in 2038 and a total cost from 2014 to 2038 of more than $7 billion. The 2014 budget request states that the increase in budget estimates for legacy contractor pensions is due to changes in demographic and mortality assumptions. In April 2011, we found that further growth in contractor pension costs could put pressure on the funding available for mission-related activities across DOE and NNSA's operations, and modernization efforts may be eroded by future increased pension costs.[31] Conversely, if budget estimates for legacy pension costs are too high, NNSA could provide additional funding for programs or reduce future budget estimates.

Budget Estimates for Two of Three Areas May Not Represent Total Funding Needed and Do Not Fully Align with Aspects of Modernization Plans

NNSA's total budget estimates may not represent the total funding needed to execute modernization plans as described in the 2014 nuclear security budget materials, and the budget estimates do not align with modernization plans in some areas. Changes in budget estimates for the stockpile area, largely due to changes in the methodology for calculating them, drove the overall increase in budget estimates for modernization; however, near-term estimates may understate the amount NNSA will need to execute stockpile plans. Budget estimates for infrastructure decreased slightly, although NNSA's long-term estimates for this area are incomplete because they do not include billions of dollars associated with early estimates for planned construction projects. Budget estimates for ST&E capabilities decreased slightly.

---

[31]GAO, *Department of Energy: Progress Made Overseeing the Costs of Contractor Postretirement Benefits, but Additional Actions Could Help Address Challenges,* GAO-11-378 (Washington, D.C.: Apr. 29, 2011).

Stockpile Budget Estimates Drove the Overall Increase Due to Changes to the Calculation Methodology, and Near-Term Estimates May Understate the Funding Needed

NNSA's budget estimates for the stockpile area from 2014 through 2031 have increased by about $27 billion compared with the 2012 budget materials, accounting for more than the total increase of $19 billion to NNSA's overall budget estimates for modernization. Figure 4 shows NNSA's budget estimates for the stockpile area from its 2012 and 2014 budget materials.

Figure 4: Comparison of Budget Estimates for the Stockpile Area in the National Nuclear Security Administration's 2012 and 2014 Budget Materials

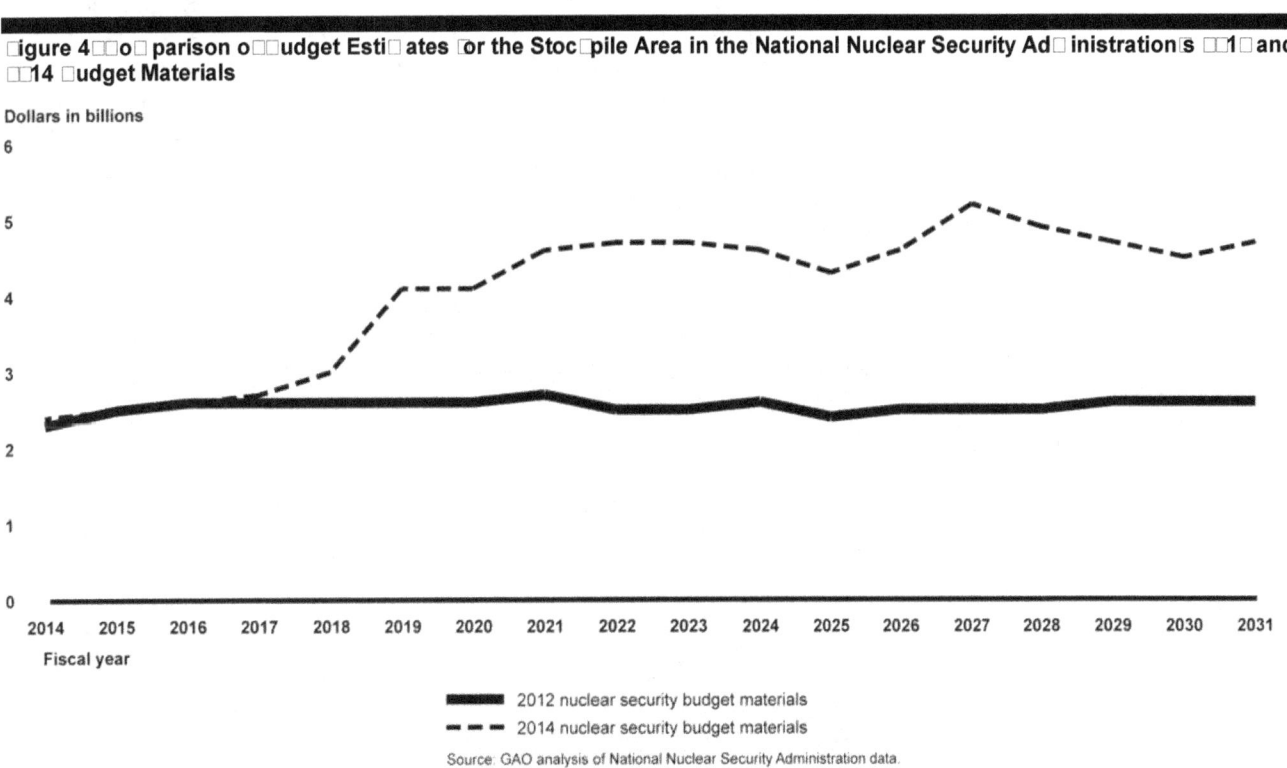

Dollars in billions

Fiscal year

▬▬▬ 2012 nuclear security budget materials

▬ ▬ ▬ 2014 nuclear security budget materials

Source: GAO analysis of National Nuclear Security Administration data.

Notes: Data are presented in current dollars.

The budget estimates for the stockpile area do not represent the total cost for maintaining the stockpile. Because of the interconnected nature of the National Nuclear Security Administration's activities, some budget estimates to support the stockpile are included in the infrastructure and science, technology, and engineering capabilities areas.

According to NNSA officials, this increase in budget estimates for the stockpile area is primarily due to changes in the way that NNSA calculated the budget estimates for LEPs.[32] NNSA officials said that the budget estimates in 2012 for the LEPs were based on data generated to execute the Reliable Replacement Warhead, a program that sought to develop a modern replacement warhead that was cancelled in 2009. NNSA officials told us that they used data from the Reliable Replacement Warhead because there was not enough data at that time from ongoing LEPs to develop cost models, and this was the best data available at that time. Starting with the 2014 budget materials, NNSA used either data from the ongoing W76 LEP to develop a cost model to generate the budget estimates for LEPs that do not yet have firm cost estimates, or actual cost estimates for those LEPs where such estimates have been developed.[33] According to the officials, this change in the estimating approach led to significant increases in the budget estimates for the LEPs, but the officials could not provide a specific amount of the increase. According to the officials, the estimates included in the 2014 budget materials are likely to be more accurate than estimates generated using the previous approach because they are based on the costs of an LEP that is in progress, rather than a program that was never executed. We did not assess the changes to the methodology for calculating the estimates or the quality of the resulting estimates because GAO has ongoing work to assess NNSA's cost-estimating practices.[34]

In addition to cost increases associated with the change in budget estimating methodology for LEPs, an NNSA official said that changes to the planned schedule for the cruise missile warhead LEP contributed to

---

[32]We could not compare the budget estimates in the 2012 and 2014 budget materials for subprograms in the stockpile area because NNSA could not provide 2012 data at the subprogram level beyond 2016, when much of the change in budget estimates in the stockpile area occurs.

[33]At the end of the second phase in the design of an LEP, NNSA publishes a Weapon Design and Cost Report that identifies baseline design and resource requirements, establishes tentative development and production schedules, and estimates warhead costs. NNSA used the cost estimates from the Weapon Design and Cost Report in its budget estimates for the three refurbishment efforts that have reached this milestone—the W76-1, the B61-12, and the W88 alteration.

[34]For preliminary observations on this topic, see GAO, *Department of Energy: Observations on Project and Program Cost Estimating in NNSA and the Office of Environmental Management*, GAO-13-510T (Washington, D.C.: May 8, 2013). GAO plans to report its final results in the spring of 2014.

increases in the budget estimates for the stockpile area. According to the 2014 SSMP, the Nuclear Weapons Council directed changes to the planned schedules for some of the LEPs to better accommodate the number and scope of all of the LEPs. In the 2012 budget materials, NNSA planned to complete the first production unit for the cruise missile warhead LEP in 2031, the last year of the period covered in the 2012 budget materials.[35] As such, NNSA included limited funding for this LEP in its budget estimates in the 2012 budget materials. However, based on its plans in the 2014 budget materials, NNSA plans to complete the first production unit for the cruise missile warhead LEP in 2024—7 years earlier than previously planned—and, therefore, an NNSA official said that the agency increased the budget estimates for the LEP in the 2014 budget materials. NNSA officials could not provide a specific amount for the increase. See figure 5 for a summary of changes to the schedules of the planned LEPs from the 2012 to the 2014 budget materials.

---

[35]The "first production unit" is the first complete warhead from a production line certified for deployment.

Figure 5: Comparison of Planned Schedules for Life Extension Programs and Major Alterations from the National Nuclear Security Administration's 2012 and 2014 Budget Materials

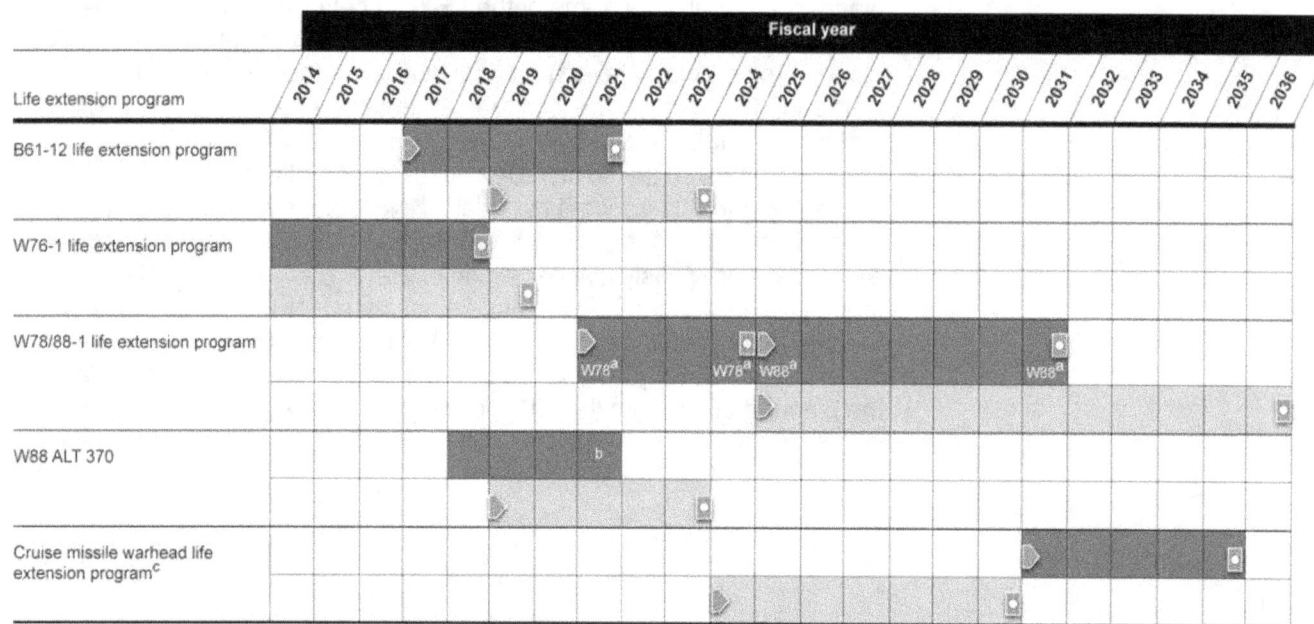

Fiscal year 2012 *Stockpile Stewardship and Management Plan*

Fiscal year 2014 *Stockpile Stewardship and Management Plan*

First production unit[d]

Production complete

Source: GAO analysis of National Nuclear Security Administration data.

[a]The 2012 SSMP discussed the W78 and W88 LEPs as separate programs, with an initiative to study the possibility of interoperability between the two systems. The 2012 SSMP did not provide schedule information for an interoperable warhead similar to that provided for other systems. In contrast, the 2014 SSMP did not provide a schedule for separate W78 and W88 LEPs. This graphic shows the 2012 plans for the separate W78 and W88 LEPs in comparison to the 2014 plans for an interoperable warhead. Based on information in the 2012 SSMP, NNSA planned to continue production of additional hedge warheads for the W78 warhead through 2035.

[b]The 2012 SSMP discussed the development of an alteration to the W88 from 2011 through 2021, but it did not provide schedule information similar to that provided for the other systems.

[c]The planned schedule for the cruise missile warhead LEP in the 2012 SSMP only extends to 2035, the end of the planning period for the 2012 SSMP. Based on the data provided, it is not clear whether NNSA planned to complete the LEP by 2035 or if production would continue beyond the schedule provided.

[d]The "first production unit" is the first complete warhead from a production line certified for deployment.

Although NNSA has increased its budget estimates for the stockpile area, we identified two areas where budget estimates do not fully align with plans and may underestimate the amount of funding NNSA needs to accomplish its modernization plans. First, separate from changes to the planned schedule for completing two of the LEPs shown above, NNSA shifted funding to 2019 and beyond for the cruise missile warhead LEP and the W78/88-1 LEP. However, NNSA officials and plans in the 2014 budget materials suggest that additional funding will be needed before 2019 to complete the first production units for the LEPs as scheduled in 2024 and 2025, respectively. NNSA included about $11.6 billion in budget estimates for the cruise missile warhead LEP and about $14.1 billion for the W78/88-1 LEP in its 2014 budget materials, but only about 2 and 3 percent of this funding, respectively, is included prior to 2019. According to an NNSA official, the total budget estimates included in the 2014 budget materials for these LEPs are accurate, but the amounts planned to be requested during the FYNSP may not be sufficient for NNSA to achieve planned program milestones. Figure 6 shows the budget estimates for the two LEPs that were included in the 2014 budget materials. According to the NNSA official, the agency shifted some of the budget estimates for the two LEPs beyond 2019 because the Office of Management and Budget approves NNSA's budget estimates through the FYNSP period, but it does not review the budget estimates beyond this period. As such, the estimates beyond 2019 are not subject to funding targets to the same extent as the estimates for 2014 to 2018.

Figure □□udget Esti□ates □or the □ruise Missile □arhead □i□e E□tension Progra□ and the □7□□□-1 □i□e E□tension Progra□

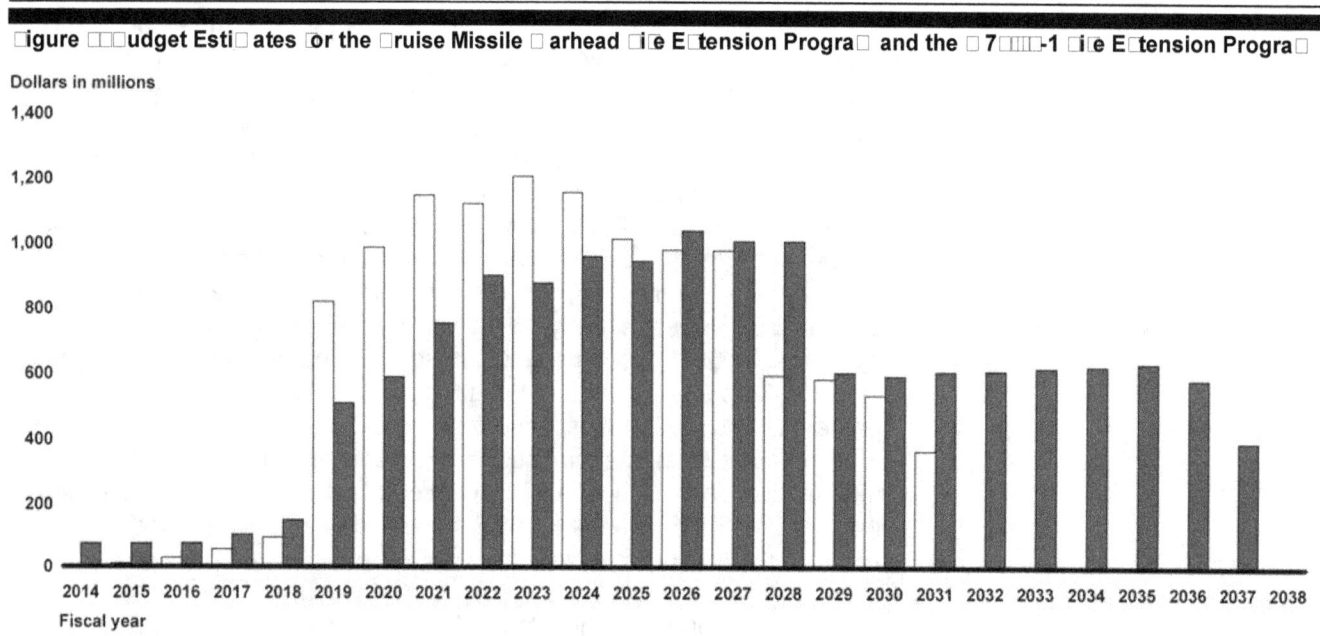

Dollars in millions

Fiscal year

Cruise Missile Warhead Life Extension Program

W78/88-1 Life Extension Program

Source: GAO analysis of National Nuclear Security Administration data.

Note: Data are presented in current dollars.

Second, the budget estimates may underestimate costs because NNSA did not incorporate contingency time to meet scheduled milestones and provide flexibility to address challenges that might arise. Our previous work on LEPs has identified that technical challenges have led to cost increases and schedule delays.[36] NNSA officials told us that there is limited contingency time in the current schedules established by the Nuclear Weapons Council for completing the five planned refurbishments to ensure that NNSA can meet the project milestones if technical challenges arise or infrastructure becomes unavailable. According to

---

[36]GAO, *Nuclear Weapons: DOD and NNSA Need to Better Manage Scope of Future Refurbishments and Risks to Maintaining U.S. Commitments to NATO,* GAO-11-387 (Washington, D.C.: May 2, 2011); GAO, *Nuclear Weapons: NNSA and DOD Need to More Effectively Manage the Stockpile Life Extension Program,* GAO-09-385 (Washington, D.C.: Mar. 2, 2009); and GAO, *Nuclear Weapons: Improved Management Needed to Implement Stockpile Stewardship Program Effectively,* GAO-01-48 (Washington, D.C.: Dec. 14, 2000).

GAO-14-45 Modernizing the Nuclear Security Enterprise

NNSA's 2014 budget materials, five of the seven weapon types in the stockpile are currently in various stages of life extension activities with work on LEPs or major alterations planned through 2038.[37] To date, NNSA has completed LEPs on two nuclear weapons: the B61 bomb and the W87 warhead. We have previously reported on these refurbishment efforts, as well as progress on the W76-1 LEP, and found that NNSA has experienced a variety of problems executing the LEPs, including schedule delays, cost overruns, technical challenges, and a reduction in the number of weapons refurbished.[38] In our 2009 report on the previous refurbishment of the B61 bomb, we found that NNSA did not leave sufficient time in its schedule to address significant technical challenges, which led to increased costs.[39] Similarly, the LEP for the W87 experienced both design and production problems that, at that time, contributed to a 2-year schedule delay and a cost increase of about $300 million.[40]

Infrastructure Budget Estimates Decreased Slightly, Although Estimates Are Incomplete

NNSA's total budget estimates for its infrastructure area for 2014 through 2031 have decreased by about $2.2 billion compared with the 2012 budget materials. According to NNSA officials, they determined the budget estimates for line item construction projects to be about $300 million per year in 2019 and beyond—escalated by about 2 percent per year for inflation—based on the amount that NNSA has typically spent on

---

[37]The W76-1 LEP is in full-scale production. Engineering development for an alteration to the W88—the W88 Alt 370—and the B61-12 LEP are under way. The Nuclear Weapons Council authorized a feasibility study for the W78/88-1 interoperable warhead LEP with study completion expected in 2016. NNSA commissioned a conceptual design study for the cruise missile warhead LEP in October 2012.

[38]A third LEP on the W80-1 was cancelled in May 2006 after DOD reevaluated its cruise missile force structure requirements.

[39]GAO-09-385. To improve future weapons refurbishment efforts, we recommended that NNSA develop a realistic schedule for future LEPs that allows the agency to address technical challenges while meeting all military requirements and build in time for unexpected technical challenges that may delay the program. In our follow-up on the status of this recommendation, we found that while NNSA has acknowledged issues and identified some steps to improve the LEP process, this recommendation will remain open and unimplemented until NNSA demonstrates successful LEP and refurbishment execution.

[40]GAO-01-48.

line item construction projects in the past.[41] To determine the specific construction projects included in modernization plans and budget estimates, NNSA requests input from the management and operations contractors each year on the specific projects that are needed at each site and uses a process to prioritize those projects within the funding available. Those projects included in the FYNSP are considered approved for project start by NNSA while projects planned for beyond 2018 are more preliminary. Figure 7 shows a comparison between NNSA's budget estimates for the infrastructure area in its 2012 and 2014 budget materials. Appendix II compares the cost estimates and schedule information provided in the 2012 SSMP to those in the 2014 SSMP.

Figure 7: Comparison of Budget Estimates for Infrastructure in the National Nuclear Security Administration's 2012 and 2014 Budget Materials

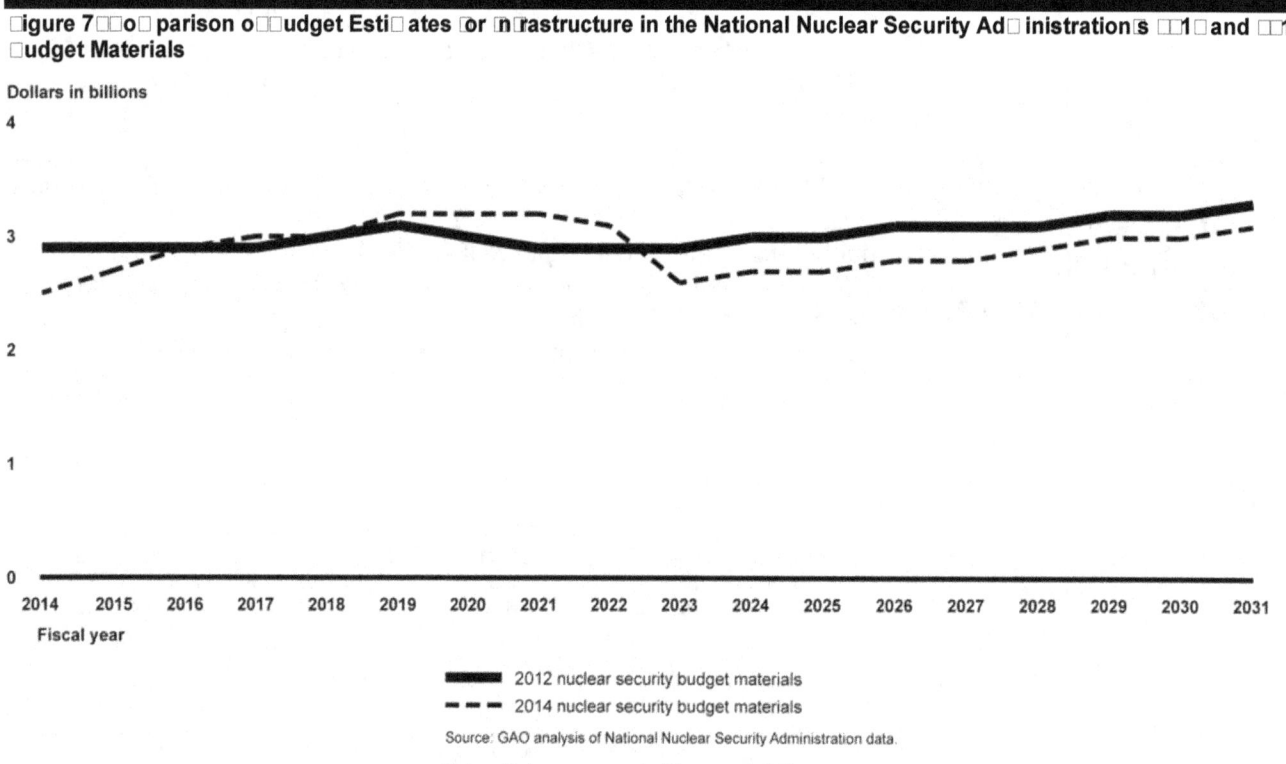

Source: GAO analysis of National Nuclear Security Administration data.

Notes: Data are presented in current dollars.

The budget estimates for the infrastructure area do not represent the total cost for operating and maintaining weapons infrastructure. Because of the interconnected nature of the National Nuclear

---

[41]Line item construction projects are construction projects for which Congress specifically appropriates funds.

Security Administration's activities, some budget estimates to support the infrastructure area are included in the stockpile and science, technology, and engineering capabilities areas.

Although NNSA's budget estimates through 2031 decline only slightly when compared with those in the 2012 budget materials, NNSA excluded most of the budget estimates for two major construction projects—the Uranium Processing Facility (UPF) and Chemistry and the Metallurgy Research Replacement-Nuclear Facility (CMRR-NF)—from its 2014 budget materials. This led to a decrease in the total budget estimates for the infrastructure area of about $4 billion for 2014 through 2031 when compared to NNSA's 2012 budget materials. However, NNSA plans to construct these facilities or alternatives to the facilities and, as a result, NNSA's budget estimates for the infrastructure area are not fully aligned with its modernization plans and likely underestimate the amount of funding that will be needed in future years. First, NNSA did not include in the 2014 budget materials any budget estimates for the latter two phases of the ongoing project to construct UPF.[42] NNSA included about $5.4 billion in its budget estimates for the first of three phases of UPF.[43] According to NNSA officials, they did not include budget estimates for the latter phases of the UPF project in the 2014 budget materials because planning for these phases of the project is still in the early stages. Additionally, NNSA did not include funding for CMRR-NF in the 2014

[42]UPF, which will be located at the Y-12 National Security Complex in Oak Ridge, Tennessee, is designed to replace all of the site's highly enriched uranium production capability currently performed in four aging facilities. The facility has yet to be built, and the first phase of the project is currently nearing a project milestone where a firm cost, schedule, and scope baseline will be established. NNSA refers to the whole facility as UPF and the three individual phases of the project as the Uranium Capabilities Replacement Project.

[43]At the request of the Senate Appropriations Committee, Subcommittee on Energy and Water Development, and in accordance with the requirements contained in the National Defense Authorization Act for Fiscal Year 2013, GAO is to report quarterly on the UPF. See GAO, *Nuclear Weapons: Factors Leading to Cost Increases with the Uranium Processing Facility,* GAO-13-686R (Washington, D.C.: July 12, 2013). In our July 2013 report on the UPF project, we found that it was unclear whether NNSA's project cost estimate of between $4.2 billion and $6.5 billion will remain valid. The National Defense Authorization Act for Fiscal Year 2013 placed a cap of $4.2 billion on the cost of the first phase of the project.

budget materials.[44] NNSA has stated the need to construct these facilities—or alternatives to these facilities—to complete its mission. According to the 2014 budget materials and NNSA officials, NNSA did not include budget estimates for CMRR-NF or its alternative because they are currently evaluating potential options for CMRR-NF or an alternative, and the plans were not yet developed enough to include budget estimates in the 2014 budget materials.[45] OMB Circular A-11 indicates that budget estimates should include the full cost of the program. Although NNSA's estimates beyond the FYNSP period may be less precise then the near-term estimates, we believe that including as much information as is known about the full cost of a program has merit with regard to future planning. In cases where complete information is not yet known, this could include a range of potential budget estimates for the projects, based on available information. Because NNSA excluded budget estimates for these two projects or their alternatives, NNSA may underestimate the total anticipated cost for infrastructure, potentially limiting the utility of the budget materials.

In addition to funding for CMRR-NF and the two remaining phases of UPF, NNSA's budget estimates for other line item construction projects planned to begin in 2019 and later may not be sufficient to complete all of the proposed projects based on current cost estimates. In the 2014 SSMP, NNSA identified 36 construction projects that sites would like to construct from 2019 through 2038 and included a preliminary cost estimate for each project in one of three ranges: (1) less than $100 million, (2) from $100 million to $500 million, or (3) more than $500 million. NNSA estimated that it would need $300 million per year, in

---

[44]CMRR-NF was expected to replace an existing facility used for plutonium-related research at Los Alamos National Laboratory in New Mexico to modernize the laboratory's capabilities to analyze plutonium and store it more securely. Originally estimated to begin construction in 2008, the project has experienced several delays and significant increases in preliminary cost estimates. In February 2012, NNSA announced that it had decided to defer construction for at least 5 years because budget constraints prevented constructing CMRR-NF and UPF simultaneously, and NNSA determined UPF to be a higher priority project. According to the 2014 SSMP, NNSA plans to phase in capabilities sooner than planned for CMRR-NF by adding equipment in existing infrastructure and is also evaluating the feasibility of constructing small laboratory modules connected to existing nuclear facilities that could accommodate higher risk plutonium operations in more modern space.

[45]We recently reported on NNSA's plans for meeting its plutonium research needs. See GAO, *Modernizing the Nuclear Security Enterprise: Observations on NNSA's Options for Meeting Its Plutonium Research Needs,* GAO-13-533 (Washington, D.C.: Sept. 11, 2013).

constant dollars, during this period for line item construction projects.[46] Using the cost ranges for the proposed projects, NNSA's plans to construct all of the proposed projects from 2019 through 2038 within the planned budget of $300 million per year are contingent on all of the projects being completed at the low end of their cost ranges (see fig. 8).[47] We found that in its planned budget NNSA can only construct its proposed projects in 9 of the 20 years of the overall construction schedule if all of the project costs are at the midpoints of their ranges and in only 3 years if all of the project costs are at the high ends of their cost ranges. Our analysis of the sufficiency of NNSA's budget estimates for line item construction projects is based on NNSA's current cost estimates. If the cost estimates for the largest construction projects increase as other projects' estimates have in the past, the amount that NNSA needs to complete all of the planned construction projects could increase significantly. For example, in our July 2013 report on the UPF project, we found that the upper bound of NNSA's cost estimate for the project has increased from about $1.1 billion in 2004 to $6.5 billion in 2012.[48] DOE remains on GAO's High-Risk List for management of major contracts and projects (those of at least $750 million) at NNSA and the Office of Environmental Management.[49] We recognize that changing the assumptions we used could produce different results and NNSA could make decisions—such as revising the budget estimates, changing the scopes or schedules of projects, or removing projects from the list—that

---

[46]Although NNSA identified CMRR-NF and the second two phases of UPF as planned projects for 2019 or later, NNSA officials told us that plans for these projects were uncertain and, therefore, no budget estimates were included. As such, we did not include these projects in our evaluation of the sufficiency of budget estimates to execute out-year planned projects, but note that additional budgetary resources will be needed to execute them.

[47]Because the proposed projects do not have a schedule for funding required in each year of execution, we assumed that 10 percent of the total cost range was needed in the first and last years of each project, and the remaining 80 percent of the funding would be needed equally across the remaining years of each project's schedule. Additionally, we used $500 million as the low estimate, midpoint estimate, and high estimate for projects in the highest cost range to provide a conservative estimate of the potential costs of the construction projects since the projects included in this category do not yet have precise cost estimates and we did not have a reasonable figure to use instead. See appendix I for more detail on the methodology we used for our analysis.

[48]GAO-13-686R.

[49]GAO, High-Risk Series: An Update, GAO-13-283 (Washington, D.C.: Feb. 14, 2013).

would change the budget estimates for a given year. Details on our methodology for this analysis are in appendix I.

Figure 8: Estimated Funding Needed to Complete Construction Projects Compared with Budget Estimates in the National Nuclear Security Administration's 2014 Budget Materials

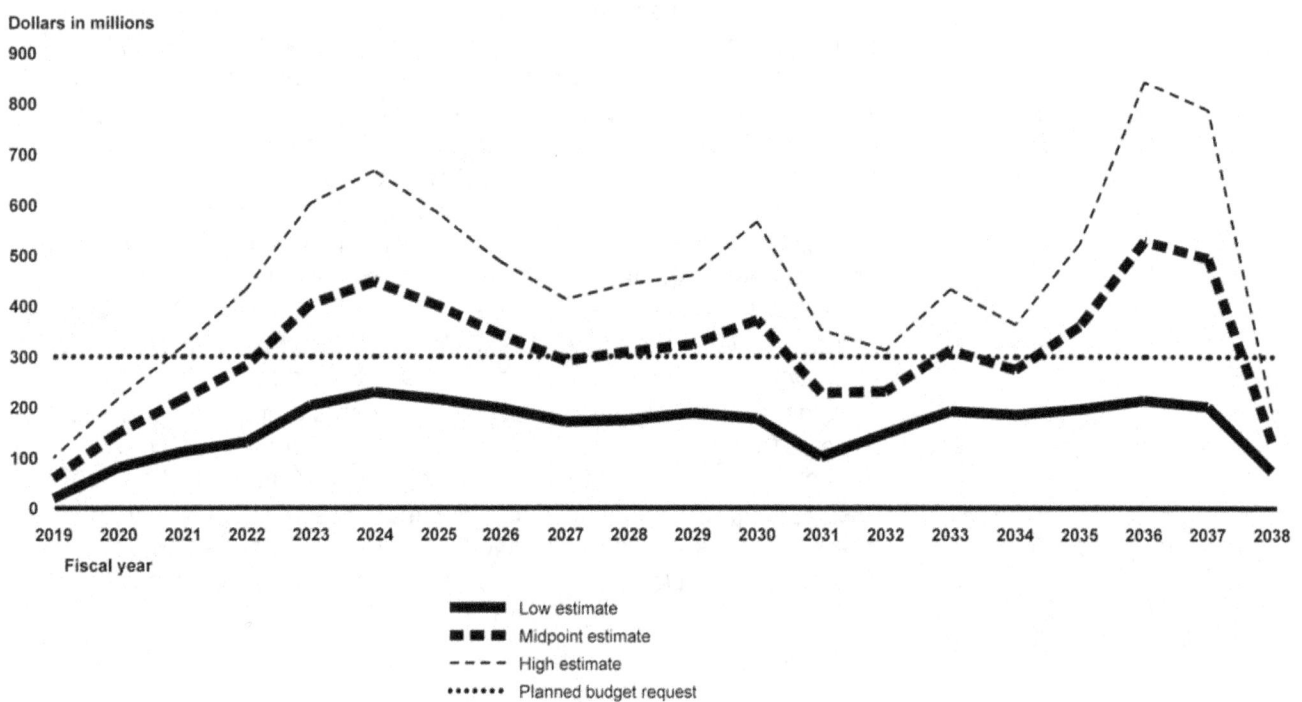

Source: GAO analysis of National Nuclear Security Administration data.

While line item construction projects are a visible and important part of NNSA's infrastructure modernization plans, NNSA anticipates spending about three times as much annually to operate and maintain its existing facilities and infrastructure as it plans to spend on construction. NNSA's budget estimates to operate and maintain its existing facilities and infrastructure remain relatively flat through 2038 at about $1.5 billion per year (in constant dollars); however, these budget estimates may not align with infrastructure modernization plans. Much of NNSA's existing facilities and infrastructure were constructed more than 50 years ago and are reaching the end of their useful lives. As a result, the agency is undertaking a number of capital improvement projects to modernize and maintain these facilities beyond high-profile replacement projects such as UPF. It may not be realistic for NNSA to assume that its annual budget

GAO-14-45 Modernizing the Nuclear Security Enterprise

estimates for operations and maintenance of facilities from 2014 to 2038 can remain flat or increase slightly (in constant dollars) when compared with what it has spent annually on maintenance activities for the past decade as this infrastructure continues to age.[50] Based on information in the 2013 updates to the Twenty-Five Year Site Plans for several sites, as the enduring facilities and infrastructure that support the nuclear security enterprise continue to age, maintenance costs are likely to grow. NNSA proposed a revision to its 2014 budget structure where sites would receive some funding for maintenance through the Site Stewardship program, but NNSA officials said that deferred maintenance projects will have to compete against programmatic priorities for funding within the overall pool of maintenance funds available.[51] These officials raised a concern that this competition for funding could lead to an increase in the amount of deferred maintenance in the future and questioned whether the overall level of budget estimates to support facilities and infrastructure maintenance is sufficient.

ST&E Capabilities Budget Estimates Decreased Slightly

NNSA's budget estimates for the ST&E area for 2014 through 2031 have decreased by about $3.9 billion since the 2012 budget materials. Figure 9 shows NNSA's budget estimates for ST&E capabilities from its 2012 and 2014 budget materials.

---

[50]NNSA changed the way it presents its infrastructure data in the budget request justification starting in 2014. Thus, for 2002 to 2013, we included funding for operations of facilities within the Readiness in Technical Base and Facilities program and operations and maintenance through the Facilities and Infrastructure Recapitalization Program in our calculation of funding for operations and maintenance of facilities. For 2014 to 2038, we included funding for the capabilities-based investments subprogram within Nuclear Programs and the site operations, sustainment, and facility disposition subprograms within Site Stewardship in our calculation.

[51]Deferred maintenance and repairs are maintenance and repairs that were not performed when they should have been or were scheduled to be and that are put off or delayed for a future period. Maintenance and repairs are activities, including preventive maintenance; replacement of parts, systems, or components; and other activities needed to preserve or maintain the asset directed toward keeping fixed assets in an acceptable condition. Maintenance and repairs, as distinguished from capital improvements, exclude activities directed towards expanding the capacity of an asset or otherwise upgrading it to serve needs different from, or significantly greater than, its current use.

Figure 9: Comparison of Budget Estimates for the Science, Technology, and Engineering Capabilities Area in the National Nuclear Security Administration's 2012 and 2014 Budget Materials

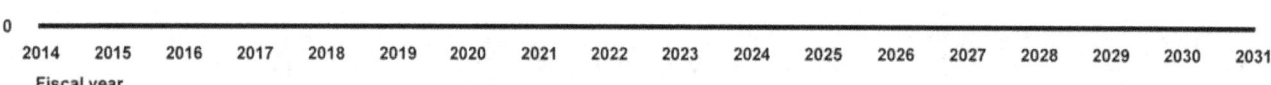

2012 nuclear security budget materials
2014 nuclear security budget materials

Source: GAO analysis of National Nuclear Security Administration data.

Note: Data are presented in current dollars.

Although the overall budget estimates for ST&E capabilities have decreased compared with the 2012 budget materials, this overall decrease masks differences among plans for specific ST&E efforts.

- The Inertial Confinement Fusion Ignition and High Yield Campaign shows the greatest decrease in estimates from the 2012 to the 2014 budget materials. Specifically, the estimates in the 2014 budget materials are $3.7 billion below those in the 2012 budget materials.
- The Advanced Simulation and Computing Campaign also saw a decrease in its budget estimates in the 2014 budget materials of $1.5 billion below the estimates in the 2012 budget materials.

In contrast, other campaigns saw an increase in their budget estimates compared with the 2012 budget materials.

- Combined budget estimates for the Engineering and Readiness Campaigns represent an increase each year of over $1.1 billion

GAO-14-45 Modernizing the Nuclear Security Enterprise

through 2031 when compared with plans in the 2012 budget materials.[52]

- Compared with the 2012 budget materials, budget estimates for the Science Campaign increase in some years and decrease in others, although the total budget estimates for the campaign increase by $171 million.

NNSA officials attributed the decreases in the budget estimates for the Inertial Confinement Fusion Ignition and High Yield Campaign and for the Advanced Simulation and Computing Campaign to changes made, in part, to reduce program costs. One change in the ST&E capabilities area is the shift in focus from ignition experiments to nonignition experiments at the National Ignition Facility.[53] NNSA did not achieve ignition—a milestone planned for achievement in 2012—through experiments performed at the National Ignition Facility and, as a result, NNSA officials said that the facility is shifting its focus to nonignition experiments and the science behind ignition in order to better understand the models which predicted that ignition would be achieved.[54] NNSA officials said that this change in focus to understanding the science behind ignition is one of the reasons for a decrease in the budget estimates. This estimated decrease in budget estimates for the campaign is also partly the result of a reduction in the level of facility operations at the National Ignition Facility and a shift of facility maintenance costs to the Infrastructure area. An NNSA official also said that the results of the joint NNSA and DOD review of resources needed for NNSA's programs anticipated that additional cuts could be made in the budget estimates for the National Ignition Facility with the expectation that, by 2018, a third of its budget could be replaced by fees paid by outside users of the facility that would be identified at a later date. This option is expected to be revisited during the preparation of the fiscal year 2015 budget materials.

---

[52]NNSA presented data for the Engineering and Readiness Campaigns together in the 2012 SSMP, but separately in the 2014 SSMP. Because NNSA could not provide data for the two campaigns separately, we combined them in our analysis.

[53]The National Ignition Facility is designed to produce extremely intense pressures and temperatures in order to try to simulate fusion conditions created in nuclear explosions, known as "ignition." Funding to operate the National Ignition Facility and conduct ignition experiments has been included in NNSA's requests for the Inertial Confinement Fusion Ignition and High Yield campaign.

[54]For more information, see U.S. Department of Energy, *National Nuclear Security Administration's Path Forward to Achieving Ignition in the Inertial Confinement Fusion Program: Report to Congress* (Washington, D.C.: December 2012).

A second change from the 2012 budget materials is the decision to slow down the replacement rate for NNSA's supercomputers. The Advanced Simulation and Computing Campaign—which supports the analysis and prediction of performance, safety, and reliability of nuclear weapons—has extended by about 1 year the amount of time the campaign plans to retain current hardware used for supercomputing, as well as slow down by 1 year the rate at which it replaces future hardware. With this change, NNSA plans to replace its supercomputers every 2.5 to 3 years instead of every 2 years. NNSA officials told us that they cannot slow down the replacement rate any further because it becomes difficult to find equipment and parts to replace or repair the equipment after more than 3 years in service.

Conclusions

NNSA faces a complex, decades-long task in planning, budgeting, and ensuring the execution of interconnected activities to modernize the nuclear security enterprise. In the current fiscal climate, providing Congress with budget estimates that reflect long-term plans and the expected funding needed to execute these plans—even if preliminary—helps in prioritizing projects and funding and aids in congressional decision making. Budget estimates reflect the administration's choices based on policy decisions. We identified several areas of misalignment or potential misalignment between NNSA's budget estimates and its modernization plans as described in its 2014 nuclear security budget materials. For example, because NNSA omitted or underestimated the costs for some areas, such as the costs of CMRR-NF and UPF or their alternatives, NNSA's future budget requests may increase compared with the estimates in the 2014 budget materials. Future iterations of the SSMP could be improved by including at least a range of potential budget estimates for projects and programs that the agency knows are needed, based on available information about these projects and programs' future costs. In addition, the budget estimates that NNSA included in some areas, such as for future construction projects, represent best case assumptions in that the agency can complete all of the planned projects only if they are completed at the low-end of the cost ranges. Moreover, because NNSA may not have incorporated sufficient contingency time in its schedules and milestones for the LEPs to address technical or other challenges, those budget estimates could further increase as well. Because NNSA is required to submit an annual budget justification and FYNSP, as well as update its SSMP, NNSA has an opportunity to continuously improve its nuclear security budget materials and bring modernization plans into full alignment with budget estimates by including a range of estimates for projects and programs the agency knows it needs in its modernization plans.

Recommendation for Executive Action

To improve the utility of future budget estimates and address the misalignment between modernization plans and budget estimates, we recommend that the Administrator of NNSA should include in future modernization plans at least a range of potential budget estimates for projects and programs that the agency knows are needed, based on available information about these projects and programs' future costs.

Agency Comments and Our Evaluation

We provided DOE and DOD with a draft of this report for their review and comment. In written comments, reproduced in appendix III, NNSA's Associate Administrator for Management and Budget generally concurred with the recommendation in this report and provided information on planned actions to address the recommendation. Specifically, NNSA plans to reflect uncertainties in program and project estimates in a budget estimates chart. NNSA believes that this action, along with other cost estimating activities that support budget estimates beyond 2019, currently provide a sufficient range of estimates consistent with the recommendation, and NNSA considers this recommendation closed. We agree that NNSA provided a range of estimated costs for most line item construction projects in the budget materials. We also recognize that similar ranges may be calculated for other programs such as LEPs, but this information is not provided in the budget materials. We continue to believe that providing ranges of potential budget estimates in the budget materials for projects and programs that the agency knows are needed could be useful in improving the utility of the budget estimates.

NNSA and DOD also provided technical comments, which we incorporated as appropriate.

We are sending copies of this report to the Secretary of Energy, Secretary of Defense, Administrator of NNSA, and the appropriate congressional committees. In addition, this report is available at no charge on the GAO website at http://www.gao.gov.

If you or your staff members have any questions about this report, please contact me at (202) 512-3841 or trimbled@gao.gov. Contact points for our Offices of Congressional Relations and Public Affairs may be found on the last page of this report. GAO staff who made key contributions to this report are listed in appendix IV.

David C. Trimble
Director, Natural Resources and Environment

List of Committees

The Honorable Carl Levin
Chairman
The Honorable James M. Inhofe
Ranking Member
Committee on Armed Services
United States Senate

The Honorable Dianne Feinstein
Chairwoman
The Honorable Lamar Alexander
Ranking Member
Subcommittee on Energy and Water Development
Committee on Appropriations
United States Senate

The Honorable Howard P. McKeon
Chairman
The Honorable Adam Smith
Ranking Member
Committee on Armed Services
House of Representatives

The Honorable Mike Simpson
Chairman
The Honorable Marcy Kaptur
Ranking Member
Subcommittee on Energy and Water Development and Related Agencies
Committee on Appropriations
House of Representatives

Appendix I: Scope and Methodology

To determine the changes to the National Nuclear Security Administration's (NNSA) plans and budget estimates, we compared the information in the 2014 budget materials to the information in the 2012 version of those materials. NNSA's plans and budget estimates are contained in two key policy documents: the agency's annual budget request justification, which contains the Future-Years Nuclear Security Program (FYNSP), which provides information and budget estimates for the next 5 years, and the *Stockpile Stewardship and Management Plan* (SSMP), which provides information on modernization and operations plans over the next 25 years.[1] The FYNSP and SSMP include information for different time frames. Specifically, the 2012 FYNSP includes information for 2012 through 2016, and the 2014 FYNSP includes information for 2014 through 2018. The 2012 SSMP includes information for 2012 to 2031, while the 2014 SSMP includes information for 2014 through 2038. Because the budget materials for 2012 and 2014 each include information for 2014 through 2031, we focused on these years in our analysis. We could not compare the budget estimates below the program level from the 2012 budget materials to the 2014 budget materials because NNSA could not provide data at that level beyond 2016. We reviewed prior GAO reports on modernization and specific programs or projects included in the plans to provide context for NNSA's plans and changes in the plans. A list of related GAO products is included at the end of this report. We also reviewed the *GAO Cost Estimating and Assessment Guide*, which highlights best practices for developing, managing, and evaluating cost estimates for capital programs.[2] We discussed NNSA's modernization plans, including areas where we identified changes in plans or budget estimates, with knowledgeable officials from NNSA and the Department of Defense's (DOD) Office of Cost Assessment and Program Evaluation.

To determine the extent to which NNSA's budget estimates align with its long-range modernization plans, we compared the budget estimates included in NNSA's 2014 budget materials with its long-range plans included in those documents. In addition to new issues that we identified as part of our review of these documents, we also followed up on the issues identified in our June 2011 review. Additionally, we reviewed prior

---

[1]NNSA expanded the time span included in the SSMP from 20 years in the 2012 SSMP to 25 years in the 2014 SSMP.

[2]GAO-09-3SP.

GAO reports to provide context for the concerns we identified and discussed areas where budget estimates did not appear to align with its modernization plans with knowledgeable officials from NNSA and DOD's Office of Cost Assessment and Program Evaluation.

We performed additional analyses to explore the extent to which NNSA could conduct projects within the proposed budget estimates. For example, to determine whether NNSA could complete the line item construction projects planned for the post-FYNSP period within the budget estimates, we used NNSA's estimated cost ranges and planned schedules for each project and calculated the amount of funding the agency would need each year to complete the projects under three scenarios: (1) all projects are completed at the low end of their preliminary cost range, (2) all projects are completed at the midpoint of their preliminary cost range, and (3) all projects are completed at the high end of their preliminary cost range. The proposed projects are not far enough into the planning process to have estimates for the amount of funding that each project will need in each year it is under way, so we assumed that 10 percent of the total cost for each project would be needed in the first and last years of the project, and the remaining 80 percent of the funding would divide evenly across the number of years in the planned schedule for each project. To help ensure that this assumption did not significantly affect the outcome of our analysis, we also performed the analysis assuming that the funding for each project was divided evenly across the number of years in the planned project schedule and found that the results did not differ significantly. For projects in the lowest estimated cost range—projects estimated to cost less than $100 million—we used $10 million for the low end of the estimate because the Department of Energy (DOE) is authorized, under some circumstances, to use certain funds to carry out construction projects estimated to cost less than $10 million. We used $500 million as the low estimate, midpoint estimate, and high estimate for projects in the highest cost range to provide a conservative estimate of the potential costs of the construction projects since the projects included in this category do not yet have precise cost estimates, and we did not have a reasonable figure to use instead. We performed a sensitivity analysis on this assumption and found that using a higher figure, such as $1 billion, for the high estimate increased the annual costs, but it did not change our conclusions, so we retained the more conservative assumptions in our analysis.

In addition, to determine the potential number of reductions of positions based on saving $240 million from workforce prioritization reductions, we obtained the average yearly salary of a DOE employee from a Congressional Research Service report on the federal workforce.[3] Additionally, we obtained data on the amount of yearly benefits that a typical federal government employee receives from a Congressional Budget Office report.[4] We inflation-adjusted the figures to 2013 dollars and added the figures together to provide an estimate of the average salary and benefits, which totaled about $150,000. We then divided the amount of cost savings that NNSA plans to attain from workforce prioritization reductions in 2014—$240 million—by the total salary and benefits. Although positions eliminated due to workforce prioritization reductions are more likely to be contractors than government employees, information on average salaries for contractors was not readily available. If contractor salaries are higher than the data used in our calculation, then fewer positions could be eliminated. If contractor salaries are lower than the data used in our calculation, then more positions could be eliminated.

We limited the scope of our review to NNSA's Weapons Activities appropriation. NNSA does not have a definition of "modernization," but NNSA officials consider all of the programs in the Weapons Activities appropriation to directly or indirectly support modernization. This scope is consistent with our June 2011 review. Additionally, we focused our review on those programs or projects with the potential to have a significant impact on NNSA's modernization plans or budgets.

All data are presented in current dollars, which include projected inflation, unless otherwise noted. NNSA's budget estimates do not incorporate reductions for sequestration. As stated in NNSA's 2014 SSMP, incorporating such reductions would lead to adjustments to future plans.

To assess the reliability of NNSA's budget estimates, we conducted electronic tests of the data, looking for missing values, outliers, or other anomalies. Additionally, we interviewed knowledgeable NNSA officials about the data and their methodologies for using the data to construct their estimates, including discussing a potential anomaly that we identified in our tests of the data. We also compared the data in the budget request

---

[3]Congressional Research Service, *The Federal Workforce: Characteristics and Trends* (Washington, D.C.: Apr. 19, 2011).

[4]Congressional Budget Office, *Comparing Benefits and Total Compensation in the Federal Government and the Private Sector* (Washington, D.C.: January 2012).

justification to the data in the 2014 SSMP to ensure consistency of the data included for the 2014 to 2018 FYNSP period. We determined that the data underlying the budget estimates were sufficiently reliable for our purposes.

We conducted this performance audit from April 2013 to December 2013 in accordance with generally accepted government auditing standards. Those standards require that we plan and perform the audit to obtain sufficient, appropriate evidence to provide a reasonable basis for our findings and conclusions based on our audit objectives. We believe that the evidence obtained provides a reasonable basis for our findings and conclusions based on our audit objectives.

Appendix II: Comparison of Planned Construction Projects in the 2012 and 2014 Stockpile Stewardship and Management Plans

The 2012 and 2014 *Stockpile Stewardship and Management Plans* (SSMP) include information on planned schedules and preliminary cost ranges for line item construction projects. Figure 10 shows the schedule and cost information for approved projects, and figure 11 shows the information for proposed projects. Approved projects are those projects that are expected to begin during the Future-Years Nuclear Security Program (FYNSP) period and have specific funding included in the FYNSP. Five of the approved projects that were included in the National Nuclear Security Administration's (NNSA) list of line item construction projects in the 2014 SSMP were not included in the 2012 SSMP. Proposed projects are those projects that are planned to begin outside of the FYNSP period. Twelve of the proposed projects that were included in NNSA's list of line item construction projects in the 2014 SSMP were not included in the 2012 SSMP. Each project has two bars of data. The upper bar for each project shows NNSA's schedule and preliminary cost ranges from the 2012 SSMP. The lower bar for each project shows NNSA's schedule and preliminary cost ranges from the 2014 SSMP. The length of the bar for each project indicates the duration of the project's schedule, and the numbers at the start and end of each bar reflect the project's planned start and end dates. Projects without a date in the first box started before 2013, and projects without an end date are planned to finish after 2038. The shade of the bar indicates the project's preliminary cost range. Projects with a light bar are expected to cost less than $100 million to complete. Projects with a medium bar are expected to cost between $100 million and $500 million to complete. Projects with a dark bar are expected to cost more than $500 million to complete.

Figure 10: Comparison of Schedule and Cost Ranges for Approved Construction Projects in the National Nuclear Security Administration's 2012 and 2014 Plans

Approved projects	Year of plan	Fiscal year (2013–2038)
Transuranic Waste Construction, Los Alamos National Laboratory (LANL)	2012	bar 2013–2017, label 17
	2014	bar to 2018, label 18
Technical Area 55 Reinvestment Phase II, LANL	2012	15 (2015)
	2014	14 (2014)
Nuclear Facility Risk Reduction, Y-12	2012	15 (2015)
	2014	16 (2016)
Test Capabilities Revitalization II, Sandia National Laboratories (SNL)	2012	14 (2014)
	2014	14 (2014)
High Explosives Pressing Facility, Pantex (PX)	2012	17 (2017)
	2014	17 (2017)
Radioactive Liquid Waste Treatment Facility, LANL	2012	13 (2013) – 21 (2021)
	2014	14 (2014) – 20 (2020)
Electrical Reliability and Distribution, Lawrence Livermore National Laboratory (LLNL)[a]	2012	
	2014	15 – 16 (2015–2016)
Electrical Infrastructure, LANL[a]	2012	
	2014	15 (2015) – 17 (2017)
High Explosives Science, Technology and Engineering, PX	2012	15 (2015) – 25 (2025)
	2014	15 (2015) – 18 (2018)
Three Emergency Operations Centers (LLNL, SNL, Y-12)	2012	20 (2020) – 26 (2026)
	2014	15 (2015) – 19 (2019)
Technical Area 55 Reinvestment Phase III, LANL	2012	15 (2015) – 22 (2022)
	2014	15 (2015) – 20 (2020)
Plutonium Facility to Radiological Laboratory Utility Office Building Tunnel, LANL[a]	2012	
	2014	15 (2015) – 17 (2017)
Fire Station, Y-12[a]	2012	
	2014	16 (2016) – 21 (2021)

(continue on next page)

Approved projects	Year of plan	Fiscal year																									
		2013	2014	2015	2016	2017	2018	2019	2020	2021	2022	2023	2024	2025	2026	2027	2028	2029	2030	2031	2032	2033	2034	2035	2036	2037	2038
Energetic Materials Characterization, LANL	2012							19				24															
	2014				17			20																			
Tritium Responsive Infrastructure Modifications, Savannah River Site[a]	2012																										
	2014				17						22																
Lithium Production Facility, Y-12	2012									21						28											
	2014			16						21																	
Weapons Engineering Facility, SNL	2012								20							28											
	2014			16					20																		
High Explosives Component Fabrication and Qualification, PX	2012									21									30								
	2014				17			20																			
Uranium Capabilities Replacement Project, Y-12	2012											24															
	2014				Phase I							25							30	Phase II and III							

Legend:

Project estimated at less than $100 million

Project estimated at $100 million to $500 million

Project estimated at more than $500 million

Source: GAO analysis of National Nuclear Security Administration data.

[a]The National Nuclear Security Administration did not include information for this project in the 2012 Stockpile Stewardship and Management Plan.

Figure 11: Comparison of Schedule and Cost Ranges for Proposed Construction Projects in the 2012 and 2014 Plans

Proposed projects	Year of plan	Schedule and cost range (fiscal year / value)
Chemistry and Metallurgy Research Replacement-Nuclear Facility (CMRR-NF), Los Alamos National Laboratory (LANL)	2012	2013 – 23 (2023)
	2014	19 (2018) – 30 (2029)
High Explosive Formulation, Pantex (PX)	2012	20 (2019) – 29 (2028)
	2014	19 (2018) – 25 (2024)
Fire Protection Building Lead-ins, PX	2012	21 (2020) – 29 (2028)
	2014	19 (2018) – 25 (2024)
MaRIE (Science Tool), LANL[a]	2012	25 (2024) – 33 (2032)
	2014	20 (2019) – 27 (2026)
Zone 11 High Pressure Fire Loop, PX	2012	21 (2020) – 27 (2026)
	2014	20 (2019) – 24 (2023)
Weapons Manufacturing Support, LANL	2012	22 (2021) – 26 (2025)
	2014	20 (2019) – 25 (2024)
Communications System Improvements, Nevada National Security Site[b]	2012	
	2014	21 (2020) – 24 (2023)
High Explosive Packaging and Staging, PX	2012	16 (2015) – 22 (2021)
	2014	21 (2020) – 25 (2024)
Material Staging Facility, PX[a]	2012	27 (2026) – 33 (2032)
	2014	23 (2022) – 30 (2029)
H-Area New Manufacturing Risk Reduction, Savannah River Site, Sandia National Laboratory (SNL)[b]	2012	
	2014	23 (2022) – 27 (2026)
Mission Support Science and Technology Laboratory, SNL[b]	2012	
	2014	23 (2022) – 26 (2025)
Non-Destructive Evaluation Facility, PX	2012	21 (2020) – 28 (2027)
	2014	23 (2022) – 29 (2028)
Research Reactor Facility, SNL[b]	2012	
	2014	23 (2022) – 30 (2029)
Cells Upgrade, PX[b]	2012	
	2014	25 (2024) – 30 (2029)
Weapons Engineering Science and Technology, Lawrence Livermore National Laboratory (LLNL)	2012	24 (2023) – 30 (2029)
	2014	25 (2024) – 30 (2029)
Plant Maintenance Facility, Y-12	2012	20 (2019) – 24 (2023)
	2014	27 (2026) – 32 (2031)

(continue on next page)

Proposed projects	Year of plan	2013	2014	2015	2016	2017	2018	2019	2020	2021	2022	2023	2024	2025	2026	2027	2028	2029	2030	2031	2032	2033	2034	2035	2036	2037	2038
Inert Machining Facility, PX	2012							20				24															
	2014														27				30								
Radiation Hardened Foundry, SNL[b]	2012																										
	2014															28							35				
Seismic Rehabilitation, LLNL	2012											24			28												
	2014																29		31								
Modern Threat Abeyance Center, SNL[b]	2012																										
	2014																29		31								
Materials Receiving and Storage, Y-12	2012											24			28												
	2014																29		31								
Applied Technologies Laboratory, Y-12	2012								21				25														
	2014																	30		32							
Fire Stations, LANL	2012													26				30									
	2014																	30		32							
Consolidated Environmental Test Facility, SNL[b]	2012																										
	2014																	30							37		
High Explosives Research and Development, LLNL	2012														27				31								
	2014																		31			34					
Consolidated Manufacturing Complex, Y-12 (Major)	2012									22										32							
	2014																			32							
Gravity Weapons Certification, SNL	2012											24			28												
	2014																			32		34					
Materials Science Modernization, LLNL	2012											24							31								
	2014																			32					37		
Robust Secure Communications Laboratory, SNL[b]	2012																										
	2014																					34			37		
12-079 Inert Storage Refurbishment, PX[b]	2012																										
	2014																					34			37		

(continue on next page)

Proposed projects	Year of plan	Fiscal year																									
		2013	2014	2015	2016	2017	2018	2019	2020	2021	2022	2023	2024	2025	2026	2027	2028	2029	2030	2031	2032	2033	2034	2035	2036	2037	2038
Receiving and Distribution Center, LANL	2012																		30		33ᵃ						
	2014																						34				
12-005 etc. Shops Replacement, PXᵇ	2012																										
	2014																							35			
Obsolete Office/Light Laboratory Building, LANL	2012																	29		32							
	2014																							35			
Mission Support Consolidation, SNL	2012											24								32							
	2014																							35			
High Explosives Special Facility Equipment, LLNLᵃ	2012														27						33						
	2014																							35			
Nuclear Security Applications Laboratory, LLNLᵇ	2012																										
	2014																								36		

Project estimated at less than $100 million

Project estimated at $100 million to $500 million

Project estimated at more than $500 million

Sources: GAO analysis of National Nuclear Security Administration data

ᵃThe 2012 Stockpile Stewardship and Management Plan (SSMP) only provides data through 2033. Projects with an end date of 2033 in the 2012 SSMP may have planned completion dates later than 2033.

ᵇThe National Nuclear Security Administration did not include information for this project in the 2012 SSMP.

Appendix III: Comments from the Department of Energy

Department of Energy
National Nuclear Security Administration
Washington, DC 20585

December 4, 2013

Mr. David Trimble
Director
Natural Resources and Environment
Government Accountability Office
Washington, DC 20458

Dear Mr. Trimble:

Thank you for the opportunity to review the Government Accountability Office's (GAO) draft report titled "MODERNIZING THE NUCLEAR SECURITY ENTERPRISE: NNSA's Budget Estimates Do Not Fully Align with Plans, GAO-14-45." I understand that the National Defense Authorization Act for Fiscal Year (FY) 2011 mandated the GAO to report annually on the extent to which the National Nuclear Security Administration's (NNSA) nuclear security budget materials provide for sufficient funding to modernize and refurbish the nuclear security enterprise (NSE). The GAO addressed (1) the changes to NNSA's budget estimates for modernizing the nuclear security enterprise since FY 2012 and (2) the extent to which these budget estimates align with NNSA's modernization plans. Based on their findings, the GAO provided one recommendation for executive action.

NNSA concurs in principle with the recommendation, and the enclosure to this letter provides our detailed response which identifies the milestones and timelines for addressing the GAO's finding. In addition, we have provided general and technical comments to enhance the clarity and factual accuracy of the report. If you have any questions regarding this response, please contact Dean Childs, Director, Office of Audit Coordination and Internal Affairs, at (301) 903-1341.

Sincerely,

Cynthia A. Lersten
Associate Administrator
For Management and Budget

Enclosure

 Printed with soy ink on recycled paper

Response to GAO Draft Report, GA-14-45
"MODERNIZING THE NUCLEAR SECURITY ENTERPRISE: NNSA's Budget
Estimates Do Not Fully Align with Plans"

To improve the utility of future budget estimates and address the misalignment between
modernization plans and budget estimates the Government Accountability Office (GAO)
recommends that the Administrator of NNSA should:

<u>Recommendation 1</u>: Include in future modernization plans at least a range of potential budget
estimates for projects and programs that the agency knows are needed, based on available
information about these projects and programs' future costs.

Management Response: Concur in Principle

NNSA currently generates cost ranges for both construction projects and life extension programs
(LEP). Section 5 of the fiscal year 2014 (FY 2014) Stockpile Stewardship and Management Plan
(SSMP), the primary document reviewed during this audit, includes general cost ranges for the
projects on the Integrated Priority List (IPL). Critical Decision 0 (CD-0) is many years in the
future for these projects.

Further, the Office of Defense Programs executes independent cost estimates for the planning
stage and major milestones of the LEPs. These provide range estimates that take into account
uncertainty in scope and schedule. The estimates are used for analysis and as planning estimates
for the SSMP and typically result in a low and a high estimate. Section 8 of the FY 2014 SSMP
only displays the low estimates.

For the FY 2015 SSMP, NNSA is currently planning to reflect uncertainties in program and
project estimates included in the budget requirements estimates chart in Section 8. In the FY
2014 SSMP, this chart used the same "low estimates" for LEPs found in that section and
programmed a non-project specific level of funding for construction for FY 2019 and beyond.
NNSA believes that the documents and activities above currently provide a sufficient range of
estimates, consistent with the recommendation, and considers this recommendation closed.

1

Appendix IV: GAO Contact and Staff Acknowledgments

GAO Contact	David C. Trimble, (202) 512-3841 or trimbled@gao.gov.
Staff Acknowledgments	In addition to the contact named above, Allison B. Bawden, Assistant Director; Cheryl Arvidson; Hilary Benedict; Bridget Grimes; and Jeanette Soares made key contributions to this report.

Related GAO Products

Stockpile

ICBM Modernization: Approaches to Basing Options and Interoperable Warhead Designs Need Better Planning and Synchronization. GAO-13-831. Washington, D.C.: September 20, 2013.

Modernizing the Nuclear Security Enterprise: Observations on NNSA's Options for Meeting Its Plutonium Research Needs. GAO-13-533. Washington, D.C.: September 11, 2013.

Nuclear Weapons: NNSA Needs to Improve Guidance on Weapon Limitations and Planning for Its Stockpile Surveillance Program. GAO-12-188. Washington, D.C.: February 8, 2012.

Nuclear Weapons: DOD and NNSA Need to Better Manage Scope of Future Refurbishments and Risks to Maintaining U.S. Commitments to NATO. GAO-11-387. Washington, D.C.: May 2, 2011.

Nuclear Weapons: NNSA and DOD Need to More Effectively Manage the Stockpile Life Extension Program. GAO-09-385. Washington, D.C.: March 2, 2009.

Nuclear Weapons, Annual Assessment of the Safety, Performance, and Reliability of the Nation's Stockpile. GAO-07-243R. Washington, D.C.: February 2, 2007.

Nuclear Weapons: Improved Management Needed to Implement Stockpile Stewardship Program Effectively. GAO-01-48. Washington, D.C.: December 14, 2000.

Infrastructure

Nuclear Weapons: Factors Leading to Cost Increases with the Uranium Processing Facility. GAO-13-686R. Washington, D.C.: July 12, 2013.

Department of Energy: Observations on Project and Program Cost Estimating in NNSA and the Office of Environmental Management. GAO-13-510T. Washington, D.C.: May 8, 2013.

Department of Energy: Concerns with Major Construction Projects at the Office of Environmental Management and NNSA. GAO-13-484T. Washington, D.C.: March 20, 2013.

Modernizing the Nuclear Security Enterprise: Observations on DOE's and NNSA's Efforts to Enhance Oversight of Security, Safety, and Project and

Contract Management. GAO-13-482T. Washington, D.C.: March 13, 2013.

Modernizing the Nuclear Security Enterprise: Observations on the National Nuclear Security Administration's Oversight of Safety, Security, and Project Management. GAO-12-912T. Washington, D.C.: September 12, 2012.

Modernizing the Nuclear Security Enterprise: New Plutonium Research Facility at Los Alamos May Not Meet All Mission Needs. GAO-12-337. Washington, D.C.: March 26, 2012.

Nuclear Weapons: NNSA Needs More Comprehensive Infrastructure and Workforce Data to Improve Enterprise Decision-making. GAO-11-188. Washington, D.C.: February 14, 2011.

Nuclear Weapons: National Nuclear Security Administration's Plans for Its Uranium Processing Facility Should Better Reflect Funding Estimates and Technology Readiness. GAO-11-103. Washington, D.C.: November 19, 2010.

Nuclear Weapons: Actions Needed to Identify Total Costs of Weapons Complex Infrastructure and Research and Production Capabilities. GAO-10-582. Washington, D.C.: June 21, 2010.

Science, Technology, and Engineering Capabilities

Nuclear Weapons: National Nuclear Security Administration Needs to Ensure Continued Availability of Tritium for the Weapons Stockpile. GAO-11-100. Washington, D.C.: October 7, 2010.

Nuclear Weapons: Actions Needed to Address Scientific and Technical Challenges and Management Weaknesses at the National Ignition Facility. GAO-10-488. Washington, D.C.: April 8, 2010.

Human Capital

Modernizing the Nuclear Security Enterprise: Strategies and Challenges in Sustaining Critical Skills in Federal and Contractor Workforces. GAO-12-468. Washington, D.C.: April 26, 2012.

Department of Energy: Progress Made Overseeing the Costs of Contractor Postretirement Benefits, but Additional Actions Could Help Address Challenges. GAO-11-378. Washington, D.C.: April 29, 2011.

Nuclear Weapons: NNSA Needs More Comprehensive Infrastructure and Workforce Data to Improve Enterprise Decision-making. GAO-11-188. Washington, D.C.: February 14, 2011.

Other Related Products

Modernizing the Nuclear Security Enterprise: NNSA's Reviews of Budget Estimates and Decisions on Resource Trade-offs Need Strengthening. GAO-12-806. Washington, D.C.: July 31, 2012.

National Nuclear Security Administration: Observations on NNSA's Management and Oversight of the Nuclear Security Enterprise. GAO-12-473T. Washington, D.C.: February 16, 2012.

Department of Energy: Additional Opportunities Exist to Streamline Support Functions at NNSA and Office of Science Sites. GAO-12-255. Washington, D.C.: January 31, 2012.

GAO's Mission	The Government Accountability Office, the audit, evaluation, and investigative arm of Congress, exists to support Congress in meeting its constitutional responsibilities and to help improve the performance and accountability of the federal government for the American people. GAO examines the use of public funds; evaluates federal programs and policies; and provides analyses, recommendations, and other assistance to help Congress make informed oversight, policy, and funding decisions. GAO's commitment to good government is reflected in its core values of accountability, integrity, and reliability.
Obtaining Copies of GAO Reports and Testimony	The fastest and easiest way to obtain copies of GAO documents at no cost is through GAO's website (http://www.gao.gov). Each weekday afternoon, GAO posts on its website newly released reports, testimony, and correspondence. To have GAO e-mail you a list of newly posted products, go to http://www.gao.gov and select "E-mail Updates."
Order by Phone	The price of each GAO publication reflects GAO's actual cost of production and distribution and depends on the number of pages in the publication and whether the publication is printed in color or black and white. Pricing and ordering information is posted on GAO's website, http://www.gao.gov/ordering.htm. Place orders by calling (202) 512-6000, toll free (866) 801-7077, or TDD (202) 512-2537. Orders may be paid for using American Express, Discover Card, MasterCard, Visa, check, or money order. Call for additional information.
Connect with GAO	Connect with GAO on Facebook, Flickr, Twitter, and YouTube. Subscribe to our RSS Feeds or E-mail Updates. Listen to our Podcasts. Visit GAO on the web at www.gao.gov.
To Report Fraud, Waste, and Abuse in Federal Programs	Contact: Website: http://www.gao.gov/fraudnet/fraudnet.htm E-mail: fraudnet@gao.gov Automated answering system: (800) 424-5454 or (202) 512-7470
Congressional Relations	Katherine Siggerud, Managing Director, siggerudk@gao.gov, (202) 512-4400, U.S. Government Accountability Office, 441 G Street NW, Room 7125, Washington, DC 20548
Public Affairs	Chuck Young, Managing Director, youngc1@gao.gov, (202) 512-4800 U.S. Government Accountability Office, 441 G Street NW, Room 7149 Washington, DC 20548